I0521563

Scan the above QR code with your phone's camera app to immediately and easily access all of Elizabeth's book-writing guides, free workshops, and programs.

"Elizabeth is a phenomenal book coach. First, there are her insights and the way she intuitively connects to her clients and makes them feel safe. Plus, she's a badass at pulling people's messages out of them."

—*Bethany Clemenson, author of* Ditching the Dream

"What an incredible guide for anyone looking to impact others through telling their story or sharing their message, even if—especially if—they don't consider themselves a writer. It's time to step into the writer you were born to be, and this book will help you do just that!"

—*Julie Solomon, business mentor and bestselling author of* Get What You Want: How to Go From Unseen to Unstoppable

"You know that thing where you're doing something really challenging and you want a friend who can pump you up, encourage you, and help keep you on track while you do it? That's Liz Lyons. WRITE THE DAMN BOOK ALREADY is the next best thing to having Liz actually sit next to you while you write. The book is full of useful information, real-life experience, and enthusiastic encouragement, all delivered in Liz's unique voice. I can't recommend it highly enough."

—Drew Linsalata, *author of* The Anxious Truth *and* Seven Percent Slower

Also by ELIZABETH LYONS

Ready or Not...Here We Come! The REAL Experts' Guide to the First Year with Twins

Ready or Not...There We Go! The REAL Experts' Guide to the Toddler Years with Twins

You Cannot Be Serious: and 32 Other Rules that Sustain a (Mostly) Balanced Mom

Holy Shit...I'm Having Twins! The Definitive Guide to Remaining Calm When You're Twice as Freaked Out

Enough: The Simple Path to Everything You Want—A Field Guide for Perpetually Exhausted Entrepreneurs

WRITE THE DAMN BOOK ALREADY

WRITE THE DAMN BOOK ALREADY

TELL YOUR STORY.
SHARE YOUR MESSAGE.
MAKE YOUR IMPACT.

ELIZABETH LYONS

FINN-PHYLLIS
PRESS

Book Cover Design: JetLaunch.net

Write the Damn Book Already/ Elizabeth Lyons.—1st ed.

ISBN 979-8-9856742-9-3 (pbk)
ISBN 979-8-9873612-1-4 (eBook)

www.ElizabethLyons.com

*For everyone who has a story to tell
or a message to share.*

In other words, for everyone.

Contents

Introduction...3

01: Welcome to the Process 17

02: Memoir Versus Nonfiction........................ 59

03: Clarify Your Why 64

04: Set Your Intention 70

05: Identify Your Core Message 77

06: Hone Your Hook.. 83

07: Become BFF with Your Reader 91

08: Create an Epic Outline........................... 103

09: Write the Damn Book Already 110

10: A Few Words On Impactful Connection.....131

11: "I Don't Know Where to Start." 134

12: "Something Came Up." 141

13: "What if People Don't Like It?" 145

14: "I'm Waiting to Figure Out the Title." 149

15: "What If I Don't Sell Many Books?".......... 154

16: "Let me Review It…One More Time." 161

17: "Is Self-Publishing 'Not Good Enough'?" .. 166

18: "What if It Doesn't Make an Impact?" 172

19: "Isn't Bestseller Status Important?" 180

20: "What Kind of Editing Will I Need?" 185

21: "Who Do I Get Feedback From."...............188

22: "How Do I Get Endorsements?" 198

23: "What About Bookstores?"...................... 204

24: Publishing Models 211

25: That's All She Wrote!............................... 229

About the Author..231

Acknowledgments 233

INTRODUCTION

H
ow long have you been thinking about possibly maybe perhaps writing a book? A few weeks? A couple of months? Sixteen-and-a-quarter years? If you're like most people I speak with—on this topic, anyway—your answer is the last option.

Maybe you've always dreamed of being an author. You remember walking through the rows of books at the public library or your local bookstore, thinking, "Wouldn't it be cool if I wrote a book that sat on these shelves one day?" Others may have suggested that you write a memoir based on your life's adventures or to flex your creative storytelling skills. Maybe you have a unique process or method you use to help people reach a desired goal, and you'd like to share that process to help more people. Maybe you've gotten excited about the new and almost limitless opportunities that abound for books to attract new clients. Perhaps you're simply wanting to be heard without anyone interrupting you to profess that you're wrong or mistaken, too this or too that, or in urgent need of counseling.

Regardless of your why (although your why is *really* important, and we'll talk more about it in a bit), you're holding this book in your hands because your interest in writing a book is, at this moment, stronger than your *dis*interest in writing a book. Your curiosity is piqued just enough. And from there, a slew of questions (no fewer than 398, in my experience) has flooded—or will soon flood—your brain, leaving you simultaneously high and numb from the combination of excitement and terror.

Because I absolutely know how this story unfolds (I've lived it), let me give you the highlights so that as you watch it play out in real-time, you'll think, "That Elizabeth knows of what she speaks!" You will then, with any luck, remember my words of encouragement and my deep desire to have your book on my bookshelf. If all goes according to plan, you will stop overthinking and get back to writing.

Highlight Number One: you'll feel super excited about the possibility of writing a book. But then, the adrenaline will wear off, and you'll go back to regular life. Until you walk down the aisles of your favorite bookstore, see another author having the kind of impact you think you could have (and know that you want), or are struck by a hilarious bit to include in the chapter dedicated to the full-blown insanity of fill-in-the-blank. For the record, this is the chapter you haven't yet written any portion of in any permanent place. But you *have* written portions of it in your head. Maybe you've orated it at dinner parties or networking meetings or to yourself while driving down the highway, hoping that everyone around you assumes you're just having a hands-free phone chat. In that moment, you'll again be high on possibilities.

Highlight Number Two: you'll think about all the people you *have* helped, just by being yourself and sharing your insights and perspective. You'll consider all the ways that writing a book could allow you to share your message with so many more people through opportunities like online courses, one-on-one or group coaching, podcasts, speaking engagements, participating in summits with some of your favorite experts, or even writing more books!

Highlight Number Three: you'll begin to imagine what you'll wear to your launch party—and then wonder if people might judge you for having a launch party. You'll wonder if anyone will show up (without yet realizing that a whole gaggle of people you don't even know will be excitedly waiting for you to arrive, because you've already made them feel so much less alone). You'll consider leather pants, taller-than-safe heels, and a new hairstyle. Maybe even purple highlights and coffin-shaped gel extension nails because, for some reason, that's a thing. You'll feel your soul start to explode from the inside out, each of your cells screaming, "Yes! This is what I want! This feels so good!"

But then, you'll come back down—not at all gradually—and wonder who will read it, and whether they'll think you've written something not-so-great, and how you'll get any Amazon reviews, and whether Sally from first grade might read it and think that the story in chapter 1 is based on her and get mad at you because of it. Or whether your mom will recognize that chapter 2 actually *is* about her and get mad at you. Or worry about how many books you'll have to sell to make back your investment in getting the damn thing published to begin with.

Highlight Number Four: if you're considering enrolling in any sort of book-writing program or writing accountability group, you will, for approximately sixteen seconds, confidently agree with everyone who declares that you are your own best investment. After all, if you don't believe in you, who will?

But then, a little voice will chime in with "Is that true? Or is that just the latest 'coach speak' to get me to invest in a program?" At this point, you'll begin to ponder whether your investment would be better spent on movies from Amazon Prime and splurging on venti instead of grande soy flat white lattes. And once again, you'll become numb to the possibilities. And on it will go.

(Sidenote: it may be the latest coach speak, but it's also true. You are *always* your best investment.)

This is how it is with book writing (and any other venture that feels a whole lot of exciting served up with a side of terrifying). Even for those who have written and published multiple books. Yes, really. But, if you stick with me, I also know how this story ends. Spoiler alert: it ends with you holding a published book—one that *you* wrote—in your hands.

Getting to a published book that you're immensely proud of isn't about getting more motivation or more hours in the day or the best celebrity partnership or literary agent. Believe it or not, two specific things will ultimately keep you from finishing and publishing your book. And those two things are: not knowing why you *really* want to write the book, and not knowing exactly what the hell the book is actually about. (It's also about not yet fully trusting your voice when it comes to writing the book, but we'll get to that too. Don't worry.)

I have strong opinions when it comes to book writing and making an impact through story, opinions that I've formed over the past eighteen years as the author of five (now six) books and having worked with hundreds of people on their own books. These opinions have little to do with the publishing space directly. I'm not opposed to any book writing approach or publishing model in existence (as long as it's executed ethically). What I'm opposed to is people not understanding what really goes on when it comes to book writing or within each of the publishing models, and therefore unknowingly making decisions without considering the unique aspects of their book project, lifestyle, and goals.

Sadly, the vast majority of people who are inspired by the idea to write a book won't get to the publishing component of the journey, because they won't ever finish writing the book! I doubt it will come as much of a surprise that I have strong theories on why that is. Not because I'm an opinionated person by nature (although some would say I am; we're all a work in progress), but because I've seen and experienced the thoughts and fears over and over again. This is why I focus so heavily within my programs on the writing piece. But I will dive into the publishing component toward the end of the book so that you at least know the critical aspects of each model to be aware of and to consider.

In the end, at least when it comes to book writing, nearly every concern can be boiled down to a fear of something, and it's important to figure out what that "something" is so we can move through it. Metaphorically speaking, we must clip the thorns from the rose to be able to comfortably hold and appreciate it. It's only through the willingness to step into that level of self-awareness and introspection that we can begin to create change—in *any* area of our lives! But most people, myself included some days, want to remove the thorns from the rose but are terrified of looking at what's really going on beneath unpleasant emotions in order to do so. Because, just like a rose, don't we require those thorns to protect ourselves? Surely, the unpleasant emotion is better tolerated than the reason that's causing it. Otherwise, we would have easily identified it and made peace with it by now. #AmIRight?

The growth that comes from deeply considering our reasons for doing anything is invaluable. In fact, if you finish this book and think, "You know what? I don't think I want to write a book after all. I thought it was going to be much more glamorous and far easier than Elizabeth is making it sound," I've done my job just as well as I did if you finish and declare, "Get out the way! I have a book to write!" If the latter is the result, I hope that this book helps you remove just one unhelpful thorn so you can get out of your own way and write the damn thing already.

I aspire to help you understand the real issues keeping you from stepping out and shining your beautiful light on everyone who's craving it, as well as get clearer on the lesser-talked-about steps involved in writing a powerful book. No, it's not all mindset work; there are tactical steps you can follow that will save you months, if not years, when it comes to getting the book written. They're the steps that most people don't even know to consider, which is why I'll lay them all out for you.

So many of the concerns that people have when it comes to writing or publishing a book are based on myths, misconceptions, and/or false expectations. And that sucks, because the result is that they stop (or never get started) based on a lie. I want you to tell your story. Hell, I want *everyone* to tell his or her story, whether it's their actual story or a story they made up when real life didn't play out the way they wanted it to. Sometimes, choosing to live vicariously through Bridget and Benjamin's whirlwind romance or Clive's hunt for the serial killer no one suspects can be, in and of itself, both healing *and* entertaining!

The process I've created over the years works best for those writing nonfiction or memoir. I'll clarify exactly what each of those is early on so you can determine which you are writing. But truthfully, many of the aspects of this process will work if you're writing fiction as well, and the information on publishing and mindset are applicable no matter the genre you're writing.

It's time to discover what's true today when it comes to being an author. Not thirty years ago when you had to "be somebody" to get a book deal. Not back in 2003 (when I first started) when the last thing you did was admit to being self-published. This book is about both the process *and* the self-discovery necessary for writing a powerful book. The self-discovery aspect is the part people talk about the least. It's amazing to discover which layers of your true self you will uncover in the process of writing a book. I promise, it's glorious.

If you want to write a book for the "right" reasons, are willing to have your expectations properly set, and are ready to enjoy the ride, I'd bet that you're going to have unexpected levels of success—even if that means you sell just over 200 books (which is reportedly the average number of books any author actually sells). Most of my clients have sold far more than 200 books because they understand these concepts and are willing to play the long game.

My own books have created unbelievable opportunities I never saw coming. I led a group for parents of twins at a local hospital, had my books ordered in bulk by hospitals for participants in preparation classes for parents expecting twins, was invited to be a guest on a "Rachel Ray Show" focused on twins and higher-order multiples, was a regular guest on local news segments, gave keynote speeches, made connections that ultimately allowed me to get my handmade jewelry line in the hands of a number of celebrities (including Kathie Lee and Nina Dobrev from the "Vampire Diaries"), launched a membership site, and ultimately became a full-time book coach and hybrid publisher.

Beyond the more substantive accomplishments, this adventure has allowed me to recognize what I'm truly capable of. If I could write a book that would go on to sell 35,000+ copies while raising three kids under the age of two, with zero connections or knowledge (at the time) of the publishing industry, I wondered what else I could do! I've gained so much confidence in my voice, my determination, and my ability to figure out nearly anything over the years as a result of writing and publishing.

Writing a book is one of the most vulnerable, healing, and expanding things you will ever do. The vulnerability comes from sharing parts of yourself you possibly haven't shared before—at least not outside your inner circle. It's healing because you'll learn to look at yourself with more compassion and awe. I promise you won't be the same person when you finish as you are now. (Don't worry; you won't be that different—just a wiser version of you with greater insights.) The expansion comes from understanding yourself, your journey, and/or your subject matter better. It can feel like mental gymnastics at times, but it allows you to become a better listener, coach, mentor, friend, and all-around human being.

Speaking of expansion, I've often spoken about the benefits of considering who you have to choose to be in a given moment in order to sit down and work your way through the writing of your book instead of cleaning the laundry room (again). What part of you presently hiding in the shadows do you have to uncover or coax out to keep moving through the challenge? Identifying that layer and bringing it to the surface is its own kind of miracle. If you're choosing to cling to the fearful aspect of yourself, you'll stay stuck, so I invite you to consider how you can choose to be brave enough to take a step toward the next best version of yourself. The answer to that, my friend, is why writing books is hard. It's not because you're climbing a mountain. It's because you're climbing a mountain you've never before climbed. You have to trust that you have within you what you need to make it to the top.

I've also spoken about who you *become* through the process of doing hard things, which is an equally valuable offshoot of any challenge. In truth, I don't believe you become anyone you aren't already, deep in your core. You already are all that you were intended to be, but in taking on challenges and striving to become more of who you are, you peel back layers that previously prevented you from fully seeing your true self. And as more and more of your full self begins to be seen, both by you and by the world, the "luckier" you get.

If you know me, you know I detest three words: can't, should, and impossible. I have a huge sign in my office that declares Everything Is Possible. And yet, I must concede that it's nearly impossible to write a book that teaches you exactly how to write a book. I wish it were simpler, believe me! But if I detailed every step *and* included suggested modifications for each person's specific situation, the book would be 1000+ pages long (and I'd probably still miss something). I'm bold, but I'm not delusional. So I'm not going to suggest that I (or anyone) can distill this process down to "9 Easy Steps." Yes, that declaration would probably sell books and programs. But it's misleading. Writing a book is hard work. It's also amazing and incredibly rewarding work.

With that in mind, here's how this book is intended to

support you on your book-writing journey.

First, I'll give you the primary considerations and steps I discuss and work through with my clients to help them write powerful, thought-provoking memoir and nonfiction. My goal is to bring your awareness to the tactical steps of book writing many people don't think nearly enough about so that you *can* think about them, which will save you time, frustration, and trips to the donut aisle or the land of "Screw this. What was I thinking?" (In my experience, the former comes right after the latter. You know, to reward myself for being so self-aware.)

Second, I'll address the questions—beyond the most common objections, which I'll address sooner—likely to keep you from writing so that you can refer to them when you're having a particular moment of "I quit." I want you to know that I truly understand what you're feeling while helping you become more confident in the process and the fact that everyone who's ever written a book has experienced the same feelings.

Third, I'll discuss the publishing process and the different publishing models available to you once you finish writing your book.

I aim to give you a well-rounded guide on the major steps of this process so that you can feel a renewed belief that you can do this (because you can), have greater confidence about *how* you'll do this, and no longer have questions that few seem to have consistent answers to living in your head, rent-free.

I'm not here to forcefully sell you a single thing. I'm here because I'm in your corner, even if only through encouraging you through these pages, in my free Facebook group where we talk about this kind of stuff all day every day, or through helpful (and sometimes laugh-out-loud relatable) posts on social media.

I'm honored to have this conversation with you. Make no mistake, I intend for it to be just that: a conversation. While I realize that this isn't, by Merriam-Webster's definition, a true conversation given that you can't respond to words in a book, you *can* pretty easily get in touch with me. I'd love to chat about your thoughts or hash out our respective opinions (as long as you're nice about it or start the conversation with something along the lines of "I respect you and your cupcake addiction tremendously, but there's this one thing you said in your book that I don't fully agree with"). Mine is not the only perspective on this topic, not by a long shot, and I'm learning more every single day about book writing, storytelling, and myself.

Without further ado, let's jump right in where all great journeys start: chapter one.

WRITE

CHAPTER 1

WELCOME TO THE PROCESS

Y ou're still here. I'll take that as a good sign. Thanks for hanging in. Now, let's get into the good stuff.

In all likelihood, you have at some point asked somebody (or one of the eighteen voices in your head), "How do I write a book?" and their answer was, "Just start writing." That used to be my answer as well, a fact I'm now embarrassed to admit because it's so blindingly unhelpful and borderline insulting. I mean, you've surely already thought of that. It's like saying, "If you want to fly to the moon, just put on a space suit." It's motivating for a millisecond, but it doesn't provide the long-term leverage one actually needs to *really* start (and keep going).

Many years ago, when people would say, "I've always wanted to write a book, but I don't know where to start," my response was: "Get out a piece of paper and a pen and write a sentence." They did, and in the span of those eight seconds, the narrative changed from "I want to write a book" to "I'm writing a book." For a few moments after hearing that, the magic in their eyes could have set the world on fire, but from there, it petered out. Quickly. And they often never wrote more than that first sentence.

Writing a book is a process, so understandably, many people say, "Well then, just give me the process!" What they mean is, "Tell me exactly what to do first, second, and third." Unfortunately, book writing is not quite that linear. But after more and more people borderline ordered me to give them the process, I acquiesced, and we'd hash out their intention, core message, target reader, and outline. You could see the enthusiasm and newfound belief coming off of them like steam on a July day in Atlanta. But then months would go by, and I'd check in with them only to discover that they still hadn't started writing. Or had stopped five paragraphs in. Because for most people, writing a book involves having a solid starting point *and* sorting through the thoughts that, even with a process in front of them, keep them in doubt.

I'd like to share a story with you because it involves my own reluctance to write a book. *This* book, to be exact. And this was after I'd already written three (if not four) books. A few years ago, I sat on a blue leather chair in a lovely Airbnb in Scottsdale, Arizona, with my legs folded comfortably underneath me, ready to start the third session of a weekend writing retreat, when Jill Daniel, founder of Happy Women

Dinners and coordinator of said retreat, looked me square in the eyes and casually demanded, "Elizabeth, *when* are you going to write *Write the Damn Book Already*?"

Truth? The idea of writing such a book did not thrill me. At all. The concept has come up time and time again, and while I've always understood why such a book might be well-received and in line with my "brand" and all that jazz, I couldn't get excited about it. The idea of writing out all the "steps" of writing and publishing a book sounded...boring. Also, difficult. Because while there are definitely clear-cut steps to *publishing* a book, the steps involved in writing one aren't nearly as precise.

Plus, let's be honest, not knowing exactly how to write a book is only a fraction of the battle. You can pretty easily find any number of 8-step programs and books that detail *how* to write nonfiction or memoir. But most people finish those programs and books and are still asking, "But *how*?" Most of those books' and programs' steps are perfectly solid. But again, what *really* keeps people from starting (and finishing) has nothing to do with not having found the perfect 8-step program. It has to do with the limiting thoughts they have about their own story or message, assumptions they make about other bestselling authors (that are wildly inaccurate), or flat-out incorrect beliefs they have about the publishing industry as a whole.

It was suggested that I take the content of my courses, put it into a book, and leave it at that. Ohmigod no. That sounded mind-numbingly monotonous, both to write and to read. And also, I couldn't stop thinking about Susie or

Jerome, fictitious names that just came to me, who would say, "Step 6 doesn't work for me because…" And their concerns would be completely valid. There are simply too many variables to speak to in one book. Additionally, because I understand how the energy of books works, I knew that if I was bored writing it, people would be bored reading it. And possibly a bit rageful. And these feelings would not compel them to sit down and write a great book.

After some consideration (read: three years of consideration), I started to rethink my attitude when it came to writing this book, and began to think more in terms of "Why this; why now?" One day not long thereafter, as I was driving down the highway, what I was really passionate about saying struck me. I'll take this opportunity to point out that having major epiphanies while driving down the highway is a full-fledged pattern for me at this point. It's how the concept behind my third book was fully fleshed out as well. What I wanted to speak to was the *full scope* of writing a book—the process *plus* the thoughts that derail people *plus* the lack of understanding of different publishing models. I wanted to tackle the topic of writing powerful memoir and nonfiction differently—and in a way that would actually be fun to consume, because I aim for *all* of my books to be fun to consume. My philosophy when it comes to books: if you aren't enjoying reading it, what the hell are you doing?

I believe strongly that if people understand how to write a powerful book *and* are supported in their shaky moments (because they're going to come) *and* understand the pros and cons of the major publishing approaches so that they can make the very best decision for their book, they can get (and stay) excited. Selfishly perhaps, this would lead to more books being written that I could purchase and read. Because I promise, I want to hear all of the stories and learn all of the things (unless it relates to cryptocurrency. I probably still don't want to learn about that).

Many people put off book writing because they believe that it requires an eight-hour-a-day commitment for eight months straight. Or they suddenly don't feel sure that they actually know what they're talking about. Or they think they need just one more certification or series of letters behind their name. Or they decide to wait until they've become friends with Reese Witherspoon so they can get her to write a testimonial (without which, they've convinced themselves that the book will go exactly nowhere). Or they fear that, more than likely, no one will ever read it anyway. Or that if someone *does* read it, it will be their mother and she'll hate it. Or it will be a perfect stranger who will have no shame about admitting, loudly, that *he* hates it, at which point their "brand" will go up in smoke and they'll have to crawl into a hole where the world has stopped spinning. We can take that last fear and go down about sixty-five rabbit holes of additional questions and concerns, all of which lead to full-on analysis paralysis and great book ideas that never make it out alive.

This is the travesty I aspire to prevent. It's why I do what I do. It's why I read like my life depends on it. Because some days, I think it truly does.

What stops most people most of the time isn't what

they say it is: a lack of information, a lack of time, or "writer's block." Actually, now might be as good a time as any to address the fact that I don't believe in writer's block. I believe that it's simply the name we give to a feeling that is the result of not knowing exactly what we're writing about or not having complete confidence that we *should* be writing about it to begin with. It's amazing to me how quickly the feeling of writer's block goes out the window once you become absolutely, unconditionally clear on why you're writing a book, what your core message is, what content you want to cover, what stories you want to include, who you're writing for, and how this book is going to be one of the most invaluable resources a reader adds to his or her arsenal of tools.

I've been asked why I'd share the key components of my programs in a book instead of "teasing it out" and then compelling people to enroll. The answer is unbelievably simple: if all you need is to get clarity on your target reader, your core message, your hook, or your outline—if that alone gets your ass in the chair day after day, writing a book you are unbelievably clear on and immeasurably proud of that you know deep in your bones is going to positively affect the life of every person who reads it—magnificent! You don't need the extra level of support I and other book writing coaches provide. But, as I said earlier, more often than not, the nuts and bolts alone aren't enough to help people get fully out of their own way, and they end up desiring some extra support in addition. Either way, I'm here to help you get the book written.

There's Just One Thing...

Before we go into the critical steps and points to consider, I want to address eight of the most common objections aspiring authors have, because I'm betting you have at least a few of them. In fact, they're likely going to sound so familiar that you'll wonder if I've been traveling around listening to the messages in your head the same way your phone obviously does. It's important to address them right away, because if we don't, they'll be sitting at the edge of your consciousness the entire time you're reading. You'll be thinking, "But I'm different because..." and therefore not fully letting the components of the process I'm going to lay out for you sink in. These objections are addressed in no particular order, because I hear one as often as another.

OBJECTION #1

"But I'm Not Really an 'Expert.'"

I hear this more from authors aspiring to write memoir than from those wanting to write nonfiction, which makes complete sense. When you've gone through something particularly challenging, it's easy to believe that without being a recognized expert on the topic or having a series of letters after your name, you don't have enough knowledge or expertise to speak about it in a public forum. I wildly disagree with this. After all, who on the planet is more of an expert on your own journey than you? I've worked with authors who have written about domestic violence, suicide, crippling anxiety, and drug addiction. Even some medical professionals and therapists don't have as much personal knowledge of the feelings and thoughts that people in those circumstances experience as the people who actually went through it! We need to read personal accounts of growth and transformation. It's the reason *Wild* by Cheryl Strayed and *Untamed* by Glennon Doyle are so wildly popular.

Books written by authors courageous enough to tell their stories about really hard journeys are among my favorites, but it's important to note that your book can have a tremendous impact even if it's far simpler or lighter in its subject matter. I've worked with authors writing about time management, redefining their relationship with alcohol, dating without losing one's ever-loving mind, finding love after fifty, and setting out to achieve borderline unrealistic goals.

When it comes to transformative nonfiction, I hear the "But I'm not a real expert" objection from experienced and new coaches/guides/leaders alike. It often stems from a false belief that without acronyms like PhD, MD, or LCSW after their name, they aren't (or won't be regarded as) a "real" expert.

You don't need a huge platform or a rocket-science degree or an overflowing bank account in order to be an expert on your topic. What you need is relevant experience and a belief in your ability to help others through sharing that experience, combined with a willingness to keep exploring your expertise while you're writing about it.

Because thoughts will undoubtedly come up that will make you question yourself. You'll have moments of "imposter syndrome" you'll need to work through. And I promise, this is where you'll grow. In most cases, you'll come out the other side more of an expert than you were when you started because of all of the self-discovery and continued deep diving into your topic you'll be doing while writing.

Now there *are* times when someone truly isn't yet enough of an expert to write a book about their topic. If, for example, you are a newly licensed nutrition coach, but you haven't worked with any clients and aren't completely sure how you'll guide your clients to remove sugar or legumes or lectin from their diet (whatever lectin is), it's going to be challenging to write a book as an expert on the topic. While you may be an expert on paper (and you may even have the initials after your name to prove it), you aren't yet an expert in the sense that you have a proven process to lay out for a reader. The reader will absolutely feel that. There's no real gauge for how many clients you have to serve or how many years you have to have studied your area of expertise before you're enough of an expert to write a book, but if you're still trying to figure out your process or your position on the main aspects of that area of expertise, you won't know what to write about, nor will you feel confident doing the writing.

You absolutely can write a book as an expert before you've worked with 87.2 clients or grown a business to $100 billion, but in order to do so while establishing yourself as a credible authority, it's critical that you know exactly what your position is on the particular topic about which you're writing. I've seen (more times than is comfortable) people whip out a book in a weekend just to "establish credibility." The minute someone gets their hands on that book, said credibility is immediately demolished because the content is so all over the place that it confirms that the author isn't yet completely sure what he's talking about or why.

Do you have to know positively everything about your area of expertise? Absolutely not! But you do need to be extremely clear on your core message (which we'll get to) and the points that support that message. This is why when people are extremely new to a specific field, they typically don't have enough material to write more than 10,000 words without repeating themselves over and over again. They simply haven't honed their experience and perspective enough to write more than that. Yet. They need more time.

One of the quickest paths from "I'm not a *real* expert" to "I actually might have some important wisdom to share" is the following exercise. Take some time to write about yourself...as though you aren't yourself. Write as though you were someone you've helped or counseled or guided in some way, or as though you were one of your closest friends (who's co-signed the idea of you writing a book based on your experience).

From their point of view, what are the unique gifts you have to offer? Why will your target readers be so well served by you writing this book? This exercise is similar to the one you've no doubt seen circulating where we ask other people (usually via social media; I'm thrilled that the trend seems to have waned) what personality trait of ours they like most or what their favorite thing about us is. We act surprised by the comments, but the truth is, if we're being honest, we're flattered but usually not completely blindsided. If someone says, "I love the way you listen deeply," we may think, "I didn't think anyone noticed" or "What a kind thing to say." Yet we can also quickly acknowledge that listening to others is important to us, and we're grateful to be doing it well enough that others have taken note.

Removing your own self-perspective (which may feel like you're bragging) and imagining what others might say about why you're the best person to write *this* particular book in *this* particular way at *this* particular time allows you to then read it back and realize, "It's not about being a bona fide expert. In fact, I never said I was one! I simply have a perspective to share and a unique way of communicating that others find valuable." That's all any amazing book is predicated on.

While writing, authors sometimes get nervous about their awareness that some of their guidance isn't their own. This is especially true if the author is a coach. I hear with frequency, "I didn't come up with this concept," and it's important to know when that's okay and when it isn't.

First of all, just as there aren't many new topics to introduce when it comes to book writing, some of the most effective mindset and growth concepts have been around for decades, if not longer. Concepts such as limiting beliefs, the shortness of time, and viewing obstacles as opportunities can be traced all the way back to Neville Goddard, Seneca, and Marcus Aurelius. Yet coaches and mentors the world over are still teaching them, and quite effectively at that. They aren't claiming the original concept as one they themselves discovered, but they're putting their own spin on explaining it further and helping their clients implement it into their lives. Explaining known concepts in a new and different way isn't where people get into trouble. Claiming those concepts as their own is. Thankfully, most people with whom I speak wouldn't dare do that.

There is a huge difference between saying, "I have a practice that I created and teach my clients. We count down, 5-4-3-2-1, and then we make a decision or take action." That's not a practice that you created; that's a practice you learned from Mel Robbins. People say, "I learned this from my coach, and it's worked wonders in my life, so I share it with my clients as well." In many cases, your coach didn't invent it either; she learned it from *her* coach. If you know who the originator of the philosophy is, absolutely credit them! I will undeniably credit whomever I learned something from, even if it was my next-door neighbor. But I'm not simply regurgitating the principles I've heard; I'm sharing how I've modified them or put my own spin on them so that they work in my own life.

Many times, my own coaches or mentors share a thought process with me, and I reply, "I've never heard of that before!" Their response: "It's not mine; I learned it from my coach." Fair enough. But for the rest of time, I'll remember learning it from them. In most cases, I've never heard of their coach, so it was my path to learn it from *my* coach (or the person standing in line in front of me at Target, who learned it from *her* coach). And so it is with your readers.

Again, it's never about claiming someone else's principles or process as your own. Do not do that! But if you're under the impression that every process of which you speak in your book has to be your unique intellectual property, please know that that's not true. It's about giving credit where it's due and trusting that the majority of your readers may not have ever heard of the concept or principle you're speaking about, because they were destined to hear about it *from you*. You are their messenger!

OBJECTION #2

"But I Don't Know if I Can Write a Whole Book."

This is a fair concern. And do you know who's blessed not to have it? People who have written a whole book (and you're about to be one of them).

The idea of "an entire book" causes a lot of problems. For one thing, people often think they have to sit down and write that entire book in one sitting. They don't consciously realize they think this way, but when they sit down to write, the writing feels "heavy," like a huge, insurmountable task.

The reason for that is that they're thinking, "I'm sitting down to work on *the book*," instead of thinking, "I'm sitting down to write a post about how to encourage kids to actually talk to their parents instead of living in their bedrooms" (for example).

You sit down and write things every day: lists, long-form posts, short social media captions, journal entries. I know that even those tasks can feel daunting at times. I know I feel that way about long-form posts. But they often feel that way because you're unsure about exactly what you want to say, how you want to organize your thoughts, or whether you're doing it "right." The exact same feelings present themselves when you sit down to write "a whole book."

As I mentioned earlier, there are a few instances when the idea of writing a whole book on a topic feels overwhelming because you perhaps cannot (or should not...yet) write a whole book on a topic. If you're writing memoir, please do not take this to mean that you need to be fully healed in order to write about something. I don't believe that to be true. There will always be new layers to uncover when it comes to healing. But you do need to be healed *enough* that you can write in a way that informs, empowers, and guides your reader.

If you're writing transformative nonfiction, and you start organic gardening in May and then decide in July that you'd like to write a book to guide others in their organic gardening journey, start taking notes on your experiences for sure, but it's probably not yet time to write a book on it.

You simply don't have enough experience and insights to fill 100-plus pages. You need to be able to say enough on your chosen topic to fill enough pages to constitute a book. And yes, opinions differ when it comes to precisely how many words that requires. My belief is that one needs to be able to write a minimum of 35,000 words on a topic in order for it to constitute a book. Are there exceptions? Absolutely. But on average, I like for those I work with to get at least 35,000 words out. Once they are clear about their core message and the outline that supports it, that becomes far easier than it may initially seem.

Sam Garcia, owner of Dirty Alchemy Digital Marketing, is an author I'm currently working with who's said to me multiple times, "I don't think I can write an entire book." In fact, she once messaged me after seeing an ad for a program that helped people write their book in one day, wondering if I'd put together such a program. Um, no. This is a person who writes voluminously for her business. I knew unequivocally that she could write an entire book (probably more than one). When she joined Book Writing Made Simple, she said, "I'm just going to take my time with this. No pressure." Within three days, she'd outlined three books (I knew she had more than one book in her!). I encouraged her to pick one book to start with, and within a few weeks, she'd written the first 20,000 words. It didn't happen in a day, and I'm hoping she now realizes how insane the idea of writing a book in one day actually is!

Another author I work with was having trouble sitting down to write full chapters, even after creating her outline.

I encouraged her think about sitting down to write "posts," not "chapters," which worked beautifully because it took the pressure off when it came to the number of words she needed to write and the feeling that it had to be "perfect." She already writes posts every single day, and she doesn't stress about them, because she doesn't have the sense that they're quite so permanent.

The first draft is just you telling yourself the story or re-minding yourself of the message in bits and pieces. Some-times, when you can sit down and just write a little blurb on the importance of a bedtime routine for babies or one sen-tence that can defuse a disagreement with a teenager, you get the starting point for great content out of your head and onto the page without feeling the pressure of needing to guide someone through the entire process of sleep training or navigating the full spectrum of human emotion during the teenage years in one writing session.

Most aspiring authors have far more to say than they give themselves credit for. As you unpack your experiences and insights, just how much content you actually have will become clear. At that point, you'll probably start worrying about which content to cut so that you don't have a *War-and-Peace*-length book on your hands by the time you're finished!

OBJECTION #3

"But I'm Not a Writer."

If I had half a cent for every time someone said, "But I'm not a writer," I'd be happily living on my own Greek island by now. Most of the people I work with don't self-identify as writers, even if they've already published a book! So when they say, "I'm not a writer," what they're really saying is, "I don't have a fancy writing degree or otherwise have a valid reason to call myself 'a writer'." It's not part of the overall identity they claim if people ask them what they do or are passionate about. But make no mistake, they're writers. They write posts and articles and blog content. They write poems and essays. They write in personal journals every single day. They write, they just don't identify as "a writer." And you don't have to identify as "a writer" in order to write a phenomenal book. It's only important that you identify as a person who has a story or message that you are choosing to share through the medium of a book.

Including this one, I've now written six books. They've been pretty well received. My undergraduate degree is in Japanese. Enough said.

When you decide to write a book, which is admittedly a larger undertaking than writing a single post, email, or journal entry (one that no one else will likely be given permission to read), it's important that you *like* to write. If you don't like to write...well...writing enough on one topic that it creates a whole book is going to be a bit of a chore (read: you're going to make it to the bottom of page 1 and declare the need for an immediate break to catch up on "Only Murders in the Building").

But also, you don't have to do the writing yourself if you really do hate writing (or absolutely, unconditionally cannot carve out the time to do it well). A huge misconception, especially when it comes to nonfiction and memoir, is that if you don't do the writing, you "cheated." Hardly. Did you know that a huge percent of bestselling books in the nonfiction and memoir categories were ghostwritten? The only challenge with this approach is that experienced ghostwriters are far more expensive than most people realize, typically starting at around $12,000 (and that's the very low end for a pretty novice ghostwriter) and going all way up to six figures. If that's not in the budget, you could hire a friend who loves to write to do the ghostwriting based on interviews she conducts with you, and hone the content later. A combined approach of talking through your points to a friend who casually interviews you about each chapter's topic and recording it so it can be transcribed and honed by you later works equally well.

While some passionate about the craft of writing might still advocate writing with quill and ink à la 1865, that alone does not an incredible book make. One of my clients recently made the observation that, by purist standards, very few of us are truly writers, given that we type our words using some software or another. I'd never given that any thought whatsoever until that moment, but it certainly didn't stop me from considering myself a writer. It's both important and beneficial to observe your own thoughts and the beliefs they've created.

Many have told me that when they sit down to write, it's like a thick film sets in atop their brain. They've got nothing. No ideas, no starting point at all. But interestingly, if I simply ask them a question about something on their outline, they start talking so fast and furious that I have to (respectfully) shut them up! They can successfully talk their ideas out, they just never considered that doing it that way when it comes to writing a book is acceptable.

Physical activity also often gets people out of their heads. Whether walking, driving, or riding their Peloton, when people get out of the energy of "The thoughts need to come out of my brain right freaking now," their opinions and insights seem to flow more effortlessly. While I don't necessarily recommend that you dictate your book while driving, you can absolutely do so while walking or working out (if you aren't too breathless). You can also have a friend ask you some questions about your outline content or your topic (especially if you're struggling with your outline) and *record the conversation*. Trust me, gems will show up. Any voice recording app will work, including the native voice recording app your phone likely has installed. You can then use a service like Otter or Rev to transcribe, clean up the transcription, and work it into a more book-friendly style.

While I'm not someone for whom dictation-while-walking has historically worked, one approach that does work for me is engaging in a mock interview. With myself. Now before I tell you how I go about this, you must promise that you won't laugh. Or, at the very least, not email me to tell me that I'm insane.

I long had a dream of being a guest on Ellen Degeneres (I know, who hasn't?). So much so that, many years ago, I took a screenshot of Ellen Pompeo and Ellen Degeneres having a conversation on Ellen's stage and photoshopped my head onto Ellen Pompeo's body. I then Mod-Podged it onto canvas and put it in my office. Hey, I was trying to man-ifest something; let me live.

Ellen is now off-air, so my dreams may have to manifest in some other way, but the strategy I'm working my way into explaining is that I sometimes imagine what questions Ellen might have asked me if I were sitting on her stage praying that a scary clown didn't pop out of the ottoman. I then answer the question, out loud. I go on for far longer than Ellen's producers would ever have allowed, but I'm certain that I could have condensed my answers if neces-sary. When I'm in this space, my answers either flow or I'm stumped. And I love it if I'm stumped, because it's an indi-cator that I need to get more clarity on that area. I either record my monologue, or I sit down and write out bullet points *immediately* afterward, when the content is still fresh.

When I think about all the incredible books the world might not have been exposed to had the author thought (or hung onto the thought), "But I'm not a writer," I get a bit lightheaded. Truthfully, whether or not you're "a writer" is sometimes determined by whether or not someone else has knighted you one, whether through a formal program or your own years of experience writing in various capacities. And sometimes, it's simply a natural gift you aren't even aware you have, precisely because no one else has ever commented on your skill in this area. While one doesn't have to be Tolstoy or Dickens when it comes to stringing together words in order to write an impactful book, some people have no idea how incredible their writing actually is.

I don't know specifically which well-known authors at one point didn't consider themselves writers (or still perhaps don't), but I know the authors I've worked with who initially made this horrifying five-word declaration. When I first connected with Cory Goodrich about her book, *Folksong: A Ballad of Death, Discovery, and DNA* and asked her to send me a few pages of the working manuscript, she quickly followed a hesitant "Okay" with "But fair warning: I'm an actor, not a writer." I almost passed out after page two, because as a writer, she was, as she stated, not good at all. She was *phenomenal*. She's an artist through and through, and whether she's expressing herself on stage or with paint or through lyrics or prose, she bleeds passion. She'd simply never had anyone read anything she'd written in order to affirm this.

Speaking of bleeding, Ernest Hemingway famously said, "There is nothing to writing. All you do is sit down at a typewriter and bleed." All of us are more than capable of *that*! So do not hang your hat on the "but I'm not a writer" rationale. No one's looking for you to be the next James Joyce, Charles Dickens, or Anton Chekhov. They're looking for you to share yourself with them and (possibly) guide them with sentences they don't have to read three times to fully absorb. They're looking for your unique voice and chosen word combinations that make your point—a point that will alter their perspective and, possibly, the trajectory of their life.

OBJECTION #4

"But So Many People Have Already Covered This Topic."

Listen, unless you're talking about anything that Elon Musk is currently working on, there simply isn't a new topic on the planet to write a book about. *Everything* has been talked about (typically more than thrice). As evidence of this, might I remark on the existence of published books titled *Salt: A World History, How to Avoid Huge Ships*, and *Don't Pee on My Leg and Tell Me It's Raining*. Not one of these is fiction. If you're worried about an "oversaturated market" in any category, let me reassure you that it hasn't happened, nor does it portend to happen any time soon.

When someone says, "I can't write about this because it's been done too many times," that's a moment in which I attempt to pivot their thought process. Most topics have been covered ad nauseam, which is why there are entire sections of bookstores devoted to them. This needn't (and shouldn't) be a deterrent! I see a saturated market as an incredible opportunity. After all, if a lot of people are talking about something, there is a reason, and that reason is called, in commercial circles, demand.

I get immediately and irrevocably nervous when someone contacts me and says, "I have an idea for a book on a topic no one has covered yet" or "This book is going to go gangbusters because nobody's ever done it." Somebody's done it. And if it's true that nobody's done it, it's an indicator that absolutely no one in the world beyond the prospective author is interested in reading something like that. The only way that's going to spark my interest is if you've figured out how to split the atom differently or fly to Mars in a week. If you've done either of those, I'm going to refer you to someone else—like NASA. Otherwise, I can all but guarantee that somebody has already done it. Is there an angle no one has yet taken? Yes. Is there an entire topic heretofore not unearthed? No. If you've identified a topic that no one has yet covered, I can all but guarantee you that it's so obscure that the market for it is between zero and zero.

If there's a large demand for discourse on a particular topic, there's going to be huge interest in different voices speaking to it. I get excited about working with an author to go into a "completely saturated" market with his or her own unique voice and perspective. The key is that you don't write about it the same way everybody else did. And the best way to ensure that you don't write about it the same way everyone else did is to simply be yourself, because there's no one else like you in the world. No matter how many times people have addressed the topic of personal growth, longevity, huge ships, or why you shouldn't pee on someone's leg and tell them it's raining (the last part of that title is completely unnecessary), the one thing no one can replicate is your experience, perspective, and insights.

Consider a fender bender on the side of the highway. You could ask fifty passersby about the incident, and nearly every one of them would describe it differently. They'll have had different feelings evoked from observing it. They'll determine someone different to be at fault. They'll have conflicting feelings about the driver of the white Tesla's bright pink mohawk. None of them is wrong, and each of them has the opportunity to influence the way you think about the incident or bright pink mohawks. Maybe you'll even be inspired to get one yourself.

For years, Brené Brown has admitted to following the advice "Write what you need to hear." I'd expand that to say, "Write what you need to hear...or what you know someone else needs to hear." And if neither of those approaches works, ask what needs to be said *through* you. This tactic can work well, because many times what makes us feel stuck is the ownership and responsibility we feel over the words coming out of us. Are they the right words? Will people respond well to them? Will they like what we're saying? Will they like *us*? When we instead ask, "What is asking to be said?" it gives our ego permission to chill out.

In the end, if everything that could be said on a topic had already been said in every way it could possibly be said, you wouldn't have the desire to write the book. New books on the topic would cease from being published. What is it that you need (or needed) to hear that no one else is saying? What is it that your target reader needs to hear that no one else is offering? It's not about rote facts and figures; it's about new perspectives and experiences.

Case in point, when I wrote my first book, now titled *Holy Sh*t...I'm Having Twins: The Definitive Guide to Remaining Calm When You're Twice as Freaked Out*, it wasn't the first book written for parents of newborn twins. But what was missing from the market (and I knew this because I was frantically searching for it and could find it nowhere) was a strategies-filled, *fun* book on the first year with twins. One that was written from the perspective of a woman who already had a baby at home, no relatives living nearby, no bottomless bank account to pull from, nary a maternity (or non-maternity) fashion bone in her body, and a determination to make it out of that first year with sanity and sense of humor intact. Similar books have successfully come onto the scene since. Their authors also chose to include pregnancy insights, were single moms, were traveling CEOs, or were intent on feeding their babies a plant-based diet. Those books were met enthusiastically by all the moms of newborn twins who identified with any of those perspectives!

When you have moments when you wonder, "Am I really adding anything new to this conversation?" return to your hook, your third-layer why, or both (explanations forthcoming). Remind yourself what *you* uniquely have to say. And remember, even though you know about all the other books out there on your topic, the general public likely doesn't. I can ask people all day how they enjoyed *Big*

Magic by Elizabeth Gilbert, and many of them will respond, "Never heard of it!" Meanwhile, an author wanting to write a book about the value and beauty of creativity is sitting at home thinking, "Elizabeth Gilbert already covered it, so why bother." Please bother, because you will be someone's Elizabeth Gilbert.

OBJECTION #5

"But How Long Is This Going to Take?"

It's an age-old question: are we there yet?

My answer will make neither you nor the three-year-old in the car happy. That answer is: I don't know; it depends. I know, you hate it (I join you in this) because it's not concrete. I know you want to know exactly how many hours you'll need to spend sweating over a keyboard before you can finally type The End and feel great about it.

I've seen people write a first draft of a book in three months. I've also seen it take three years. The timeline depends on a variety of factors, including but not limited to how dedicated you are to a writing schedule, how clear you are on your topic, and what else is going on in your life. Here's what *doesn't* necessarily affect the timeline: how good of a writer you are, how good your message or story is, or what anyone else says about how long writing a book "should" take.

A better question to ask than "How long will it take" is: Why is it important for me to know how long it will take?

I've identified two primary motivators for this question. One is that people want their expectations set. That's completely fair. We like to have a general idea of how long things will take so we can plan for them. If I'm invited to join someone on a road trip, I want to know approximately how long it's going to take to get from Point A to Point B. But some experiences simply don't have a definitive or reliable timeline. There are people who would love to have us believe that we can build a 7-figure business in twenty-one days or find our soulmate with a simple 13-step system, but I would argue that while the process they propose may be sound, the alluring timeline attached to it isn't, necessarily.

It's important to realize that not finishing the writing of your book (or hitting seven figures in your business or falling madly in love) in a specific timeframe does not mean that anything is wrong with you or that you are doing something incorrectly. Everyone's timeline is uniquely their own and, as such, is perfect. Both a three-month and a three-year timeline can produce an incredible book. Knowing this allows rule followers and more competitive folks to relax a bit and lean into what will surely be an incredible experience, no matter how long it ends up taking.

If, on the other hand, it's important for you to have a timeline because you're thinking, "If I can't do it in three weeks, I don't want to do it," you *might* want to reconsider this whole book-writing thing. If someone says, "I want to build a multi-million-dollar business, but only if I can do it in six months," not many people will encourage that (the exception being anyone who has a program that teaches people how to go from zero to seven figures in three weeks). Same thing if someone says, "I want to be able to play tennis like Serena Williams, but I only want to take four lessons" or "I've battled major anxiety all my life, but I want to find the one perfect meditation that will alleviate it immediately and forever."

When statements like these are boiled down, the truth is laid bare: the person wants the end result (don't we all!) but isn't interested in climbing the mountains and navigating the speed bumps that present themselves along the way. They aren't passionate enough about both the end result and the growth *and* life lessons experienced along the way to stay committed.

In conclusion, it'll take as long as it takes. And it will be worth every minute.

OBJECTION #6

"But Now Just Isn't the Best Time."

One of the first things people have to make peace with when starting to write a book is that book-writing is not an overnight process. It's an adventure that can be both incredibly rewarding *and* overwhelming at times. Even if you're not writing about yourself, at the end of the day the words and the message that you are putting out there come *from* yourself. Therefore, you are exposing something, even if only your storytelling ability.

Most of my clients write memoir or nonfiction infused

with story, so in some way, shape, or form they're writing at least pieces of their own story. Because it can feel a bit scary to do so, it's completely normal to find yourself saying, "I just don't think it's the right time." And you know what? You're right. Because when it comes to writing a book, it's both always the right time and never the right time. Kind of like having kids. Or eliminating Kit Kats from your diet.

That said, there are a few times when I'm prone to agree that it's not the right time. If you're in the middle of (or about to embark upon) a cross-country move, about to welcome triplets, or not sure what you really want to write about (as in, your ideas run the gamut and range from navigating challenges to pickleball techniques to automobile maintenance), it's perhaps not quite the right time—just yet—to write your book.

But if you get really honest with yourself and discover that the reason it's "not the right time" is no more complex than you're afraid of people's reactions, of your own ability to communicate your story in words, or of any aspect of the "how" of book writing or publishing, I can almost assure you that this is the perfect time! Because you're about to show yourself exactly how much you do know, how much you are capable of, and how very wrong you are about what others are going to think.

OBJECTION #7

"But What If It's Not Good?"

Let's agree on one thing, shall we? The word "good" is wholly subjective. Many people think Picasso's work is brilliant and worth millions of dollars. I feel like it's quite basic (and I say this as someone who cannot draw even a stick figure well). Many people went wild over Elizabeth Gilbert's *Eat, Pray, Love*, while many others said less-than-kind things about it. Lots of people will take any chance they get to wrap one fried food around another fried food, while others shudder at the very thought.

"Good" has next to nothing to do with the artist or creator, and everything to do with the person consuming their creation (and the mood they're in when consumption commences). When we're in a space where we're concerned about whether or not something is "good," there's another question to ask ourselves that's far more effective: "Did I put my entire self into this?" If the answer is yes, it's going to be received as not just good but outright incredible—by someone. Not everyone, but someone. And that someone is who you're writing for. It's never going to be "good" by everyone's standards. There are people who don't think that Sprinkles cupcakes are good, for God's sake.

Remember that "good" is in the eyes of the beholder. Focus on putting your whole self into it, and know that it's going to resonate so deeply with someone that you'll rue the day you spent time wallowing over this question.

OBJECTION #8

"But What if I Make Someone Angry or Hurt Their Feelings?"

It's incredibly common for there to be a piece of your story that you're nervous about telling (whether it's part of your personal life or your business life). In business, people sometimes worry about upsetting someone to the point that they'll be sued. In personal life, people also worry about hurting someone else's feelings (or upsetting someone—say, an ex) to the point that they'll be sued.

I'm not an attorney, but I've guided authors through this a number of times. In so doing, I've learned a number of lessons when it comes to how to write about other people's involvement in your experience without causing a problem that requires deep breathing, a change in address, or expensive lawyers. There is always a way to include aspects of your experience that involve another human being, no matter how emotion-charged that experience might have been or continues to be. So that I've said it, if you're truly concerned about the litigiousness of your story or the way you're telling it, please consult with an attorney who's well-versed in this area prior to publication.

You have the right to tell your story. You have a right to your perspective, experience, and feelings. You have a right to communicate it as just that: *your* experience, perspective, and feelings. What you do *not* have is a right to someone else's story (meaning, you do not have the right to express *their* experience, perspective, and feelings) or make assumptions about why they did something, make declarations about their character, or label them. This can be a challenging part of not just telling your story but working your way through it, because as human beings, we have an innate need to be right and to be confident that we weren't even two percent the cause of our own distress.

Here's a good way to know the difference between labeling or diagnosing others and sharing your experience. If you're writing a book about dating, and you want to have a chapter about how to deal with narcissists, you can say, "Two decades ago, I dated a narcissist." What I advise against is saying, "Two decades ago, I dated a narcissist. His name was Bobby Bruhaha, and last I checked he's still pretty active on Tinder, so beware."

Writing about an ex-partner or spouse can be heavily challenging because many of your readers will know to whom you are referring. I therefore advise you to be careful when it comes to needing to share the pieces of your experience that might help the reader versus sharing pieces of your experience that persecute the other person (in a medium that doesn't allow them the opportunity to tell their side).

Consider which portions of someone else's involvement were critical to the point you're trying to make. Getting down in the depths of things someone else said or did not only creates a potential problem for you, but it can also take your reader down *your* emotional journey in a way that's off course from how you intend for the book to help them. It's typically not necessary to go too deep into the layers of what another person did, or why you believe they behaved in that manner. You aren't in a court of law (nor do you want to end up in one), and you don't need to prove to anyone that you're right or they're wrong. You aren't writing the book to be validated or vindicated, or so that others will say, "You poor thing! You put up with so much!" (If you *are* writing for that reason, you want to work through that before you write the book.)

No, it's not enough simply to change the name of the offending party. If you're speaking of an ex-spouse or a parent or a son (and you only have one son), changing names won't be enough to give the person anonymity. If you give enough identifying information about someone for a reader to clearly recognize who you're speaking about, and the information you're giving could jeopardize that person's ability to earn income in some way, you could be at risk of being held liable by them. But there's no reason to end up there. You simply never need to go that deeply into another person's actions in order to make the point you desire to make.

Ask yourself how much of the story is about the other person and their choices versus how you handled it, responded to it, or reacted to it. The best ratio is about 90/10, with ninety percent of your content devoted to how you reacted, and ten percent devoted to the details of their involvement. It's almost always the easiest approach to place blame on someone else, but when we own our choices, we show the reader how they can do the same while taking action toward the resolution they seek. We have no control over other people, which is a huge component of what's causing so much angst in your reader (and *caused* so much angst in you!). When you can shine a light on that discomfort for the reader by acknowledging that you truly understand their perspective, the growth opportunity you provide them is invaluable.

Some helpful starting points to consider when writing include:

- "What I felt was..."
- "What it meant to me was..."
- "What I learned was..."
- "I responded by..."

I've worked with authors where, through editing their first draft, it became clear that they were still very angry at someone from their past who was a critical component of their story. As you're writing, ask yourself whether you're telling the story in such a way that the lens through which the reader will see the experience is yours or someone else's. If you're narrating your perception of someone else's perspective, it's a sign to pause and reassess. When you focus on someone else's behavior, you give your power away *and* you lose your state of Powerful Vulnerability (which I'll explain in detail in chapter 10).

Very few people enjoy being at an event where they're forced to listen to a speaker they came to learn from, but who stands on stage and whines for an hour about all the things someone else did to them. When you spend more time in the telling of the story *behind* how you got to the emotion, perspective, and positive action that came from it, you lose the opportunity for the experience to transform your reader. In some cases, you lose them altogether, because as a result of dragging them into your drama, they get annoyed and decide to pick up another book. Without realizing it, you're giving all the glory to an individual you don't even like! Share just enough to bring the reader to the point of "I see what you've been through."

Again, no one can tell you that you didn't experience or feel something. They can't tell you that your perspective or feelings are wrong. As long as you stick with what *you* felt and how *you* moved through it, you'll be just fine.

When it comes to concerns about hurting someone's feelings through the retelling of a story or of someone's involvement in a painful aspect of your experience, especially in a day and age when so many people are engaged in or hearing about inner child work, people get confused about how much is too much (or too little) to share. Perhaps when you were fifteen, you experienced something with a parent that you later identified as having caused your abandoned child archetype to come out more often as an adult. You wonder, "If my parent reads the book, will they be hurt? Or livid?"

While you are not responsible for how someone else receives the information related to your experience, I advise that if you care about the person with whom you had an emotionally charged experience that you're sharing, sit down (or have a phone call) with them before the book comes out. Let them know that you're writing a book, and you need to share this particular revelation because you truly believe it will help your readers. Clarify that you aren't sharing it to be unkind or hurtful, and that you're clear in the book that you don't blame that person. Many people do this very effectively! They share a story about something that happened when they were young and either preface or follow it with something along the lines of "To be clear, my parents are incredible people and they loved me tremendously."

Knowing where your heart is and what your intention is in sharing the details of an experience can help to avoid many of concerns you may have while simultaneously shedding light on areas for which you may need to seek greater healing. Having such a conversation with someone can also provide a great opportunity for each of you to come to a place of understanding. The goal isn't to get their permission to keep the content in the book. What it dredges up for them in terms of feelings is for *them* to work through. It's simply out of love and compassion that you're letting them know up front.

If they have a really strong reaction, maybe you decide to handle the story differently in the book. Oftentimes, overtly stating that they were the participant in the experience isn't necessary to get your point across, nor is it worth the stress that creating friction in your relationship will cause. But I encourage you to make this decision based on what's best for who you are choosing to be in this moment, not in order to people-please or placate someone else. That only allows any resentment to stick around (if not grow).

Another important point is that you don't always have to clarify the role of the person who said whatever they said in order to make your point. Let's say it was your mom who said something that impacted you when you were younger. You could easily say, "When I was fifteen, a key figure in my life said such-and-such to me, and it created a thought that I was not good enough. That thought stuck with me for many years." You don't have to directly state that the person who said whatever they said was your mother. *Who* said it is often irrelevant (unless you're writing a book on mother/daughter relationships).

Remember, the first draft is just you telling yourself the story or reminding yourself of the message. Allow yourself the grace to have a cathartic moment when necessary. If you're exploring an experience or topic that is emotionally charged for you—that causes you to feel sadness, anger, or frustration—you will likely become activated when writing about it. Perhaps you haven't ever written about it, or maybe you haven't thought about it in a long time. Or maybe, every time you think, talk, or write about it, you become activated. That's okay. When you notice that it's happening, let it happen. Those are feelings that need to come out. But once you finish yelling or crying onto the page, go back and hone it in order to remove the excess anger, sadness, or frustration. Sometimes you'll have to go through chapters many, many times to be able to pull that emotion out. Occasionally, you may need to with a therapist, coach, or mentor in order to further work through a challenge.

When you commit to doing the healing and taking back that power, you expand, simply because you're reclaiming the energy. In order to be powerfully vulnerable, the energy around the experience has to be cleaned up before it stays in the book or is presented publicly. This doesn't mean the issue never bothers you again. You're always welcome to sit with a friend and vent about what a lousy son of a bitch someone is. Having those feelings doesn't make you an imposter when you write about it or speak about it publicly. You simply get to a point where there is an aspect of you that can go deep into the feeling and feel it, and there is an aspect that can be powerfully vulnerable about it. (Again, I'll talk more about how to be powerfully vulnerable in chapter 10).

Your reader is looking for you to say, "I went from here to here. And in that time, there were a lot of peaks and valleys. If I had known how to have a different approach, I could have alleviated some of the time it took and some of the pain I felt while going through it." They want you to minimize *their* time in overwhelm and fear, and they believe that you can do that, because you've been navigating through something for a longer period of time than they have at this point.

A FEW MORE ENCOURAGING WORDS

Book writing, like marathon training, starts out strong. (I can only assume this; I assure you I haven't trained for a marathon, nor do I have plans to.) You've got all the excitement and momentum in the world. You're doing this. It's happening. And then...

I want to warn you about this now so that if (read: when)

it happens, you can simply think, "Elizabeth said this would happen. I'm normal." Certain thoughts are likely to show up, and those thoughts are going to say things like, "What are you doing?" "Why are you doing this now?" "Maybe you need more time to figure out your process" and "This feels very chaotic and discombobulated; clearly I don't have a message to share." When this happens, please remember that it's not a sign that it's time to quit. It's an incredible opportunity to respectfully tell the thoughts in your head to shut the hell up, get in the back seat, and hold on for the ride.

Even when you have an outline acting as a roadmap through this process, the more you write, the more you'll have moments where the content of what you're writing feels all over the place. You'll begin to question your message, your commitment to the project, and at times, your overall sanity. The only people this doesn't affect are people who have already written a book. It *happens* to them, it just doesn't affect them, because they know to expect it and how to write through it.

Make no mistake: you are writing your way *through* the message. You are sorting the components of it. You are *excavating* a book by intentionally setting out on an exploratory mission to uncover exactly what you want to say, as well as why and how you want to say it. You are taking years of experiences, thoughts, perspectives, and feelings and sifting them through the filter of "Does this have a place in this book?" Not recognizing how normal (and beneficial) this is not only stops people from starting, but it also causes thousands to quit when they start feeling concerned that maybe they don't have a message after all or know what they think. About anything.

Writing a book is an enormous exercise in patience. I'm the most impatient person on the planet, so this was an unfortunate realization for me to have. However, given my stalwart resistance to it, if I can learn to exercise patience in this area, I trust that you can too. Book writing is a process. It's important to detach from the belief that other people's process is quicker, more linear, and blessed with a greater up-front understanding of where the book is going at all times. Every author who has written an incredible book—including *your* favorite books, whether fiction or nonfiction or memoir—goes through this.

Will it all ever come together? Absolutely. But you cannot have an expectation of exactly when that will be. I know, this sucks. You must simply continue to recommit to the doing. To a willingness to untangle all of your experiences and perspectives and be excitedly curious about which of them you need to think through just a bit more in order to become clearer about what you want to say about it. In so doing, you will grow your perspective, expertise, and confidence by leaps and bounds. You will become much clearer about who you are and what your message is through writing the book. That is a *good thing*! If you're a coach, speaker, mentor, or course creator, doing this work will make your content better and far more effective. Don't allow yourself to think that how quickly or easily you write the book is an indicator of how valuable your content is, how well you know yourself or your process, or whether you're truly ready to share your message. It's not.

Writing the book is an opportunity for you to grow further into your beliefs, processes, and experiences, as well as how you choose to guide others through them. Even with straight memoir (which has no explicit how-to component), there will be moments when you're writing about something and think, "I don't know if I truly know why I made this particular choice." This isn't an opportunity to shrink. It's an opportunity to take a step back in order to contemplate and get clear. So that you can blossom.

Allow the book to come through you as opposed to forcing it to come out of you. This is a subtle but important distinction. When we're in a place of force, our words carry that energy all the way to the reader. The best way to get into a place of allowing your words to flow through you is by getting extremely clear on your core message, your magnetic writing voice, and your target reader (which is exactly why those are three parts of the process I'm going to walk you through).

Finally, don't get caught up in details such as a "magic" final word count, the perfect number of words to write each day, or adhering to a writing schedule that doesn't feel great. As far as word count goes, many people automatically think a book has to be 80,000 words in length. That number comes from the traditional publishing world, when books were, on average, that long. However, that statistic takes into account works of fiction, which are notoriously longer than nonfiction. It's entirely possible to have a

50,000-word book that's extremely thought-provoking. Quality over quantity is the goal.

Most of the time, a book needs 20,000 words just to have a spine. I encourage my authors to shoot for at least 35,000 words, and most of them end up writing between 50,000 and 60,000 when all is said and done. Adding in unnecessary words or repeating details in order to hit a specific word count does not a powerful book make. Make sure each word counts.

Now that we've put the most common objections on the back burner, at least for now, let's dive into the good stuff.

CHAPTER 2

MEMOIR VERSUS NONFICTION

The authors I work with are primarily writing nonfiction or memoir. Because it's common to wonder, "Wait, what's the difference between fiction, nonfiction, and memoir again?", perhaps it would be helpful for me to clarify this before we go much further.

In short, fiction is a made-up story. It's the latest Colleen Hoover, Emily Henry, or Annabel Monaghan novel you can't wait to curl up with on the couch on a rainy Sunday (or, let's face it, a sunny Wednesday afternoon).

Nonfiction and memoir are cousins, and the most significant difference between the two when it comes to writing them can be found in the author's intent. I work with authors who are writing what I refer to as transformative nonfiction or inspirational memoir. The intention when it comes to transformative nonfiction is to guide the reader toward a specific transformation. The author has a very specific set of steps or a specific process they'll guide the reader through in order to help him or her reach the stated goal. Examples of transformative nonfiction include *Atomic Habits* by James Clear, *The 7 Habits of Highly Effective People* by Stephen Covey, and *The 5-Second Rule* by Mel Robbins.

Inspirational memoir, on the other hand, is simply the telling of a specific moment, lesson, or insight from someone's perspective in order to inspire the reader. Of key importance is the fact that the author is not attached to the specific way that the book inspires or moves the reader. What the author is focused on is telling the story of her journey through a particular experience, with the hope that some portion of it may inspire the reader. Great examples of inspirational memoir are *Wild* by Cheryl Strayed, *The Glass Castle* by Jeannette Walls, and *Folksong* by Cory Goodrich.

There can absolutely be crossover between the genres. Many times, people who are writing transformative nonfiction include a good number of stories. Sometimes, people write memoir with a bit of prescriptive direction. (The former is more common than the latter.) Please don't get caught up thinking you must fit neatly into the transformative nonfiction box or the inspirational memoir box. What's most important is identifying whether or not you desire for your book to provide clear direction on the steps your reader can take or simply share an experience and allow them to discern for themselves what, if anything, they choose to take from it.

One question that often arises is: "When is one genre more effective than another?" Another way I hear this question posed often involves the word "should." "Should I write memoir instead of nonfiction?" or "Should I have a multi-step process in order for my book to be most effective?"

One thing you'll quickly learn about me is that I'm quite sensitive to the word "should." Whenever anyone uses the word when assessing the approach they'll choose (in any area of their life), I'm a firm believer that they're not thinking from the standpoint of what they really want to do. They aren't trusting their own inner voice and desire. When someone asks which style of book they *should* write, it feels disingenuous to answer with anything other than "Which do you want to write?" Yes, I answer a question with a question sometimes. That's just how it works.

I truly can't give people the answer they most deeply desire, which is to say that I can't tell anyone that one genre is outright more impactful or effective than another. What I can do is help someone sort through which style of book they genuinely want to write. You can determine the answer for yourself without me, simply by asking yourself two questions. The questions are: "When I think about sharing my message, how do I feel when I consider simply telling the story and having no attachment to how the reader receives it or acts upon the information?" And "How do I feel when I consider giving the reader a step-by-step plan or general process for reaching their desired outcome?" Most people have a visceral feeling of comfort when it comes to one option and a tightness when it comes to the other. Trust that feeling!

Plenty of people have written memoirs that strongly impact readers. Plenty have written nonfiction books that do the same. You know what's also true? Many people don't like memoir. And many others don't like nonfiction. Hell, many people don't like reading at all, and don't even get me started on the plethora of die-hard opinions when it comes to print versus digital verses audiobooks! What's most important *isn't* identifying which style will be more loved across the board, because the answer is: neither—especially if you're writing in a particular way simply because you think you should. I promise, given the popularity of the medieval cosplay genre, I can assure you that you can find people who will love your book, no matter what style you write it in. No, I don't know if medieval cosplay is an actual genre, but I'd be surprised if it isn't and can almost guarantee that something similar exists (and is wildly popular).

It will be far more likely that the reader will love it if you actually enjoy writing it. If you don't, that displeasure will be easily felt by the reader. If you're just trying to "get it finished" so you can get it into the world, your reader will feel that too, and you'll lose them by page fifteen. Even great books sometimes struggle to keep a reader's attention amidst the plethora of "read this next" emails and social media posts, which is why it's more important than ever that your book be written with heart and intention in order to truly stand out.

Now that you have a more thorough understanding of the different genres and have (hopefully) gotten clearer about which feels more aligned given your topic and intended delivery, let's hop into the next step of this adventure: clarifying *why* you're writing a book to begin with.

CHAPTER 3

CLARIFY YOUR WHY

Knowing why you're writing your book—why you're *really* writing your book—is of paramount importance. While I love hearing people's answers to "Why do you want to write a book?", there are two that immediately concern me.

The first is, "So many people have said I should write a book." Having someone else believe so much in the power of your story or your process that they tell you that you should write a book about it is, no doubt, a huge compliment. But as we've already discussed, if you aren't firm in *your* why when it comes to writing a book, not only will the writing feel challenging, but you'll struggle heavily when it comes time to market it.

A second answer that gives me pause is: "It'll provide a nice passive income." I don't believe passive income is even really a thing. I mean, if you aren't talking at all about something you're selling (or you haven't hired someone else to do the talking), you probably aren't selling much of it. A book provides passive income in the sense that if someone randomly comes upon it and buys it, you make a few dollars. But most people need far more than a few dollars each month to pay all their bills, so when the month ends and you're staring at all the bills, are you going to say, "No worries! The passive income from the book I never talk about will cover it"? Probably not.

This is why one of the first areas I address with my authors isn't their book topic, their title, their subtitle, or their platform size. It's *why* they're writing the book they're writing. The conversation goes beyond what you want the book to do for you and what you want it to do for the reader. It focuses on three specific questions: why *this* book, why *now*, and why are *you* the one to write it?

Book marketing is a long game. And it's a much more fun one (from where I'm standing anyway) when you're clear on the answers to these questions, because there are so many ways you can get the word out (pun intended). If Plan A doesn't work well, you move to Plan B, and so on. Most people make the majority of their book-related money from the byproduct of their books (coaching, courses, speaking, and so on), not from book sales alone. And again (I'll say it until I'm blue in the face), you have to have put your energy into writing a solid book to begin with.

I recently had a new client ask me, "Will it be worth it?" I thought she was referring to whether she'd make back her investment in the program, because this is what most people are referring to when they ask this sort of question. Upon clarification, she was wondering if she'd actually do the work required to get a great book written. In her mind, if she didn't, *that's* why it wouldn't have been worth the investment. I quickly shifted the conversation by asking, "What kind of decision are you willing to make with regard to this project? And, to clarify, I'm not talking about a decision about whether or not to invest!"

I've watched people invest three figures in a program and go all in, and I've seen people invest multiple five figures and do absolutely nothing. There's a bit of a messed-up notion floating around the coaching space lately that suggests that investing just to get around the energy of a program (or a coach) will, in and of itself, be highly transformative. I think that, said in that way, it's a very coach-serving statement, and left out of the conversation is the fact that it's not just about making an investment. It's about making a *decision*.

When you make a decision to write a book with a clear understanding of the answers to "Why this book? Why now? Why am I the one to write it?" you stack the will-I-actually-get-it-done deck in your favor. Take the time to dig deep enough to clarify precisely why you're doing this. I refer to this as getting clear on your third-layer why, and the clarity you receive will all but ensure your follow-through. Anything less is akin to the values assessment exercise people engage with, wherein they initially state that their family is their most important value but then admit that they rarely prioritize spending time with their family. But for people who are crystal clear that their family is their top priority—they're living it, not just saying it—a discrepancy between words and actions simply doesn't occur. Similarly, once you've tapped into your soul's deepest desire when it comes to writing a particular book, it's quite difficult to tap out of it.

I'll illustrate the reason I believe that an author's ultimate why is three layers deep, using this specific book as the basis (since I know the answers). We start with the first layer: *Why do I want to write THIS book?* The first-layer answer is related to the top-level problem you want to solve. My answer: I want to share my perspectives on writing memoir and nonfiction so more people can get out of their own way, share their experiences, and impact others.

We then go to layer two: *Why do I want to write this book, in THIS way?* The second-layer answer speaks to your unique angle and to what your reader doesn't know that he or she doesn't know when it comes to solving their problem. My answer: Giving people "8 simple steps" is easy, but most of the time, having those steps doesn't lead to a written book, because the author's thoughts get in the way. I believe it's important to focus on the "energetic" aspect of writing a book in addition to the tactical aspect. It's high time people dive deeper into the energetic/mindset aspect of book writing so we can get more powerful, transformative messages into the world!

Finally, we get to layer three: *Why do I want to write this book in this way?* The third-layer answer speaks to your belief (also expressed as passion or core value) when it comes to why you are so passionately committed to helping people solve a specific problem (or understand a specific experience, if you're writing memoir to raise awareness of a systemic or societal issue). My answer: I believe that stories change the world for the better, one person at a time, and if more people know exactly how valuable their stories are *and* know how to get them into the world and grow into higher, more whole versions of themselves while doing it, the world becomes a better place. That specific layer: **stories change the world, and if more people tell theirs, the world becomes a better place——my world becomes a better place** is not only my third-layer why, it's the core motivation that keeps me writing a particularly challenging chapter. It keeps me disciplined to my writing routine. It's tied directly to my soul's desire, not my ego's desire, and my soul's desire will always be the pull that's most difficult to argue with.

To give you another example, my client Michelle Runnels is a parenting coach for moms. We recently uncovered her third-layer why when it comes to her decision to write a book as part of her way of serving moms in the trenches.

Her first-layer why is: "I want to write a book to help moms navigate their relationships with their 'tweens, teens, and young adult children——kids they *know* are great but who they hate sometimes." (I nearly spit out my coffee when she expressed it this way because it was just so...relatable!)

Her second-layer why is: "I want to help my reader understand that, even though she thinks otherwise, her kid isn't the problem. *She's* the problem." For the record, this probably isn't something she'd say on the back cover or in her title. Her target readers deeply believe that they're not the problem, and it's important to ease them into her belief that they are, and do so in a way that doesn't offend them or cause them to say, "Oh *hell* no!" right from the get-go. Her ability to subtly help her clients accept this and make shifts that get them to their desired outcome is what makes Michelle's coaching style magical.

Her third-layer why is where she gets really passionate (which happens for most people, and it's the reason getting to it is so valuable). It is: "I believe that motherhood is the ultimate opportunity for women to grow psycho-spiritually."

So, why are you writing *your* book? What's *your* third-layer why? Take some time to get clear on this before moving on to Chapter 4. I promise, the more energy you put into clarifying your why, the more solid the foundation will be onto which you'll place the results of the next step: setting your intention for the book.

SET YOUR INTENTION

Knowing your *why* for writing the book and setting your intention for the book are two different things. Related, yes, but subtly different. And both are equally important to assess.

Your why has to do with your reason for writing the book—the deeper, soul-led belief or value that compels you to share your story or message. Your intention for the book, on the other hand, has to do with what you want the book to do *for* you. There are nearly endless options when it comes to how your book can serve you (and that's a good thing!), but in my experience, listing out your top eleven is exciting at first and debilitating not much later. Honestly, how does one start a podcast, take over the public speaking circuit, and woo Kathie Lee and Hoda at the same time? (The answer is: not successfully.)

I realize it may feel odd to focus on yourself—not your reader—first, and it's a bit contrary to what a lot of book coaches advise. For the record, this doesn't mean that those other coaches are "wrong," only that I've found an alternate sequence to be more effective. For sure, we will, in short order, turn our focus to your reader, because doing so is incredibly important. But in my experience, when authors aren't clear about what *they* want first, they sometimes end up with what looks to outsiders like a glorious outcome, while the author is left feeling a bit like "This wasn't exactly what I wanted to happen here. But no one ever asked me about what I wanted." In addition to managing your emotional response to the book's trajectory, knowing what you want the book to do for you (and visualizing accordingly) will actually help you be more efficient and strategic when it comes to the writing.

Even when I'm clear about emphasizing the word "you" when asking, "What do you want the book to do for *you*," the answers I typically receive include variations on "I want people to feel better about their situation," "I want people to realize they aren't alone," and "I want to inspire people to make a change in their life." All valid and noble responses (although they need to be clearer, which I'll address in Chapter 6), but they speak to the *reader's* benefits, not the author's.

I believe that the reason people answer that way is, again, it can feel quite uncomfortable to respond in what seems to be a selfish manner. Trust me; do it anyway. Being clear about what *you* want from this book will impact the way you write it and the energy you bring to it. If, for example, you know from the outset that you want to create a course based on the core principles of your book, you can be thinking about course content and delivery as you're writing. You can consider how your book might lead into a course and how that course will take the principles explored in your book to the next level.

Alexandra Hill, who is an empty-nest coach for moms, gave the concept of marrying book content with future course and program content a significant amount of consideration as she worked on her outline. She knew she wanted to expand her one-on-one coaching practice into a group program, and she quickly identified the ways she could expand upon her book content through exercises and other face-to-face practices she could incorporate into her coaching programs. It helped her feel a strong sense of continuity between what she was already offering and what she could add in over time, and she got incredibly excited seeing how much opportunity there was for her to expand her offerings and the many ways she could increase the ways she'd serve people beyond the book.

If you're still wondering how a book can so easily lead to greater personal and professional opportunities for you, consider the last time *you* were blown away by a book and wanted to know more about the author. You likely found and followed them on social media, and if they had a program, podcast, or downloadable guide, you possibly signed up for that as well. It's one of the least expensive and most accessible ways to let people know who you are, what you're about, why they can trust you, and how you can help them. Authors who write nearly every genre, from memoir to nonfiction to fiction to poetry to manga, attract new followers and fans every single day. No fancy billboard or social media ads strategy required.

Other ways authors want their book to benefit them personally/professionally include:

- Paid speaking engagements at industry events
- Private coaching programs
- Group coaching programs
- Online courses
- General societal awareness
- Having one's voice heard/speaking one's truth
- Hosting summits or retreats
- Speaking at luxury resorts/wellness centers (both nationally and internationally)
- Attracting new members to a Facebook group or other community
- Creating a membership program
- Hosting a podcast focused on the book's main topic
- Attracting new patients (physicians, nutritionists, chiropractors, and other medical professionals)
- Bulk sales to corporations, book clubs, subscription boxes, conference attendees, and the like.

Once you identify a variety of ways you can envision your book expanding your personal and/or professional opportunities, take it one step deeper and clarify your top three wants. For example: host a podcast, create an online course, have a one-on-one offering. Then, narrow that list of three down to one. What is the *first* way that feels incredibly exciting to get your message out? Not "What *should* I do first?" Not "What's likely to generate the most income the fastest?" But "What *excites* me the most?" The reason this is important to do is that, again, it's not easy to create a course, a podcast, and a one-on-one coaching program simultaneously and do them all well—especially if you don't have a large team supporting you. When you plan to start with just one, you'll identify book content to expand upon for course content or possible podcast topics or exercises for your clients. It makes the book-writing process more productive overall. And, as a bonus, it helps to remind you that your book is, more often than not, a *component* of your overall business, not your be-all-end-all product.

Before we move on from this topic, let's touch upon an aspect of authorhood that people are *real* resistant to talking about: money. While talking about money is uncomfortable for a lot of people, I encourage you to be open to getting more comfortable with it, if necessary, because part of the equation when assessing what you want your book to do for you does involve how much money you want the book to make, directly or indirectly. I want to help you feel more comfortable contemplating this, because it's incredibly important that you are completely honest with yourself when delivering your final answer.

I've heard my fair share of authors say, "I don't really care about making money off the book. I just want to help others." And then, when the book doesn't sell more than fifteen copies (because they posted once about it—or not at all), they're suddenly frustrated because they "aren't going to recoup their investment." If you want to make money from your book (directly or indirectly) because you are providing value with the intention of *serving*, there is nothing wrong with that. For some, the goal is simply to get their message into the world, which is wonderful. But once the book is released and isn't generating significant monthly paydays, I often receive messages from those same authors that express something to the effect of "Why isn't the book making money? Does that mean it isn't good?" My first question is typically, "Just so we have a starting point from which to begin this discussion, when was the last time you posted about or emailed your list about your book?" The answer, nine times out of ten, is "I don't know. Several months ago?" or "I'm supposed to have an email list?"

If you want to make money from your book, directly or indirectly, *own that*! I find that people who are at all altruistic are often incredibly uncomfortable declaring that they want to be paid to help people. It's as though we think that martyrdom is the key to every castle and kingdom. It's not. We all exchange monetary currency every single day for products and services that make our lives better. I relentlessly and gladly give my money to every coffee shop within fifty square miles of me, and they give to me in return the value of joy in a twenty-ounce cup. If you identify with a thought that says, "If I'm helping people, it's wrong to desire compensation for it," get that thought out of your head. Or, at the very least, do what you need to do to work through where that belief came from and whether you want to continue to hold onto it.

All that being said, there are people who truly don't care if they make any money from the sale of their book. But even when that's the case, the question remains: How will you get your message into the world in order to help others if that is your primary goal? If the book lives in obscurity, how many people will you help? Whether you want to make money through book sales and/or programs and services that complement your book, consider what feels good to you when it comes to getting your book out there. No answer is inherently right or wrong, good or bad. It's all about what feels exciting to you. And the answer to that can absolutely change as time goes on.

CHAPTER 5

IDENTIFY YOUR CORE MESSAGE

One of the foremost concerns for every single author who's ever considered putting pen to paper in order to tell his or her story is: *Does my story actually matter? Is it really that special?*

Here's the thing. Just as there aren't many (if any) topics that haven't already been covered, there aren't many truly unique journeys. And somewhat ironically perhaps, this is *exactly* why stories matter. If only one person had ever lost someone to an illness or been involved in an almost plane crash or discovered that the yellow Jolly Ranchers are actually the best ones, the story's magnificence would both be born and die with them. No one else would care. The reason stories matter is that we relish the opportunity to say, "Oh my gosh, I thought I was the only one!" We crave the knowledge that we aren't alone in our feelings about death or heights or being given the wrong flavored candy.

What is unique is the way you experienced whatever you've experienced. If you send five people to the middle of Nebraska, they're all going to experience it a different way. There could be five essays written on the experience, and if the readers didn't know better, they might not even know that all five people were in Nebraska to begin with. If you surveyed one hundred people who attended a Beyoncé concert—even who all had VIP tickets—each would have a different way of describing the concert: its sights, sounds, smells, the fact that she didn't sing "Single Ladies," and the way they were inspired to live their lives differently going forward. They'd each also have a unique way of describing their experience at the concert. Some of their descriptions would resonate with some people, while other people would resonate more strongly with the descriptions given by other attendees. In similar fashion, what makes a book unique isn't the message itself but the author's unique way of putting his or her experience into words. That's something no one else in the universe can replicate. And it's why every single story matters.

Another fact, however, is that in order for one's story to make the desired impact, someone has to be compelled to buy the book, start reading it, and keep reading it. The best way to ensure that you attract the people destined to do this is by being extraordinarily clear on your core message. In nonfiction, the core message can be boiled down to the type of transformation the author can provide for the reader. In memoir, it can be narrowed to a specific insight gleaned, lesson learned, question answered, or challenge overcome by the author.

To make this even clearer, I'll give you some examples. In *The 5-Second Rule* by Mel Robbins, the core message is inarguably...wait for it...her 5-second rule (what it is, why it works, and how to implement it into your life). In *Everything is Figureoutable* by Marie Forleo, one can safely assume that the core message is that...again, wait for it...everything is figureoutable. The book goes on to explore that belief in greater detail and show readers how to apply it to their own lives.

As you've no doubt just gathered, once an author figures out the core message, that message often becomes the title or subtitle. This is a great reason not to hitch yourself to a title before you do the lion's share of the writing. More often than not, a new (and far better) title than the one the author has been banking on and doodling on pretend book covers for months (or years) emerges as the writing is happening.

The core message doesn't always make its way to the title, of course. The core message of *Happy Days* by Gabby Bernstein isn't necessarily happy days, per se, because that's rather vague. In this case, the core message is about getting from trauma to personal freedom and inner peace (which is, in fact, the subtitle). For my fifth book, *Enough: The Simple Path to Everything You Want—A Field Guide for Perpetually Exhausted Entrepreneurs*, the core message is how to get off the mental hamster wheel of go-go-go-get-get-get-when-can-I-stop-please-I'm-really-tired as an entrepreneur.

When writing memoir, the core message is often a bit less "tangible" in the sense that it's not typically expressed as "how to get from this place to that place." However, it's as succinct as if it were. *Wild* by Cheryl Strayed has a core message of resilience and growth after the death of a parent. *Love Warrior* by Glennon Doyle has a core message of love conquering all. *The Mother of All Makeovers* (by my brilliant client, Hollie Gyarmati) has a core message of navigating the unexpected, losing one's identity, and rebuilding into something greater. To be clear, I haven't spoken with any of the above-referenced authors to confirm whether they agree when it comes to the core message they were intending (besides Hollie), but I'm keeping my assumptions high-level enough that I don't think any of them is too big a leap to make.

In hindsight (meaning, once the book has been written), the core message of a book is incredibly clear to the author (and everyone else). It's in the initial stages of idea contemplation and outlining that it's harder to discern (and often, narrow down) the core message so that the author is clear about what she's focusing on within that book. It's not uncommon for an author to feel like she has a large amount to say about a wide variety of topics, and even about a single topic. Without getting clear on the core message, it's easy to veer off course and begin to feel confused, overwhelmed, and like maybe this book writing idea wasn't such a great idea after all. And that's the worst part, because I can assure you, once the idea of writing a book takes hold, it likely won't let go. Your soul wants you to write this book, and it will absolutely help you get clear on what this specific book is about, if you allow it to.

The core message of your book can usually be expressed in fewer than eight words and stated as "getting from _____ to _____" or "getting from _____ to _____ as a (parent/entrepreneur/business owner/dog lover)." The core message isn't the same as the hook, which is also brief but allows for a bit more information. (I'll talk more about the hook in a bit.) For now, it's incredibly important to simply get clear on your core message. Also, getting clear on your core message isn't for anyone but you. Your core message doesn't have to be shared with your entire social media circle. It's merely intended to help you put boundaries around what points you'll make and which stories you'll tell.

If you're writing nonfiction, what is your book's main focus? In other words, why would a reader (who isn't your mother, your best friend, or the best friend of either of those two people) purchase your book? What problem are they trying to solve? What solution are they looking for or hoping to understand better? What habit are they trying to break? What need or desire are they seeking to fill? What goal are they trying to accomplish? When you combine what you want to say with what your reader wants to hear about, you've got the recipe for an incredibly powerful book.

A great example is *Deep Work* by Cal Newport. The core message of this book is the value of deep, focused, undistracted work. He backs up his claims with both science and personal experience. Because that's the core message, he doesn't share many (or any) childhood stories about getting lost at the playground or developing a preference for ice cream in a bowl, not a cone. If a piece of content doesn't relate to the core message in some meaningful way, it likely doesn't have a place in the book.

If you're writing memoir, what is the challenge you've overcome, the insight you've gleaned, the lesson you've learned, or the question you finally discovered a transformative answer to? When you can combine what you want to share with a journey your reader is curious about—even if they don't need to know the exact steps you recommend when it comes to that journey and don't need to have experienced what you've experienced in order to be curious about your experience—you've set the stage for an impactful book.

A solid example of a strong, clear core message when it comes to memoir is *Eat, Pray, Love* by Elizabeth Gilbert. The book was written as a documenting of sorts of her journey to heal herself from a spiritual crisis. What she did brilliantly was incorporate her wit into the content, which not all authors do or have to do. But if you have it and are writing about deep emotional turmoil, it can add a degree of levity that compels the reader to not only root for the author but fall madly in love with her at the same time. That second part allows for a felt connection that can soften the reader's edges enough to consider that perhaps, just maybe, even if she can't go to Italy or Bali, she can incorporate some of Gilbert's insights to shift a portion of her own life.

CHAPTER 6

HONE YOUR HOOK

Identifying your core message helps you create and hold a boundary around your book's content. Your hook is a bit more potent. Knowing your hook is critical for three reasons. First, it helps you get clarity on how your book stands out amidst the sea of other books written about the same topic or personal journey. Second, it keeps you on track when you're outlining. Third, it gives you a succinct response you can confidently deliver when someone asks, "So what's your book about?"

Think of your hook as your "elevator pitch." I remember when I first learned about elevator pitches. It was a business world concept, and the gist was that you only had as long as a two- to three-floor elevator ride to explain to someone your business concept in a way that got them intrigued. The very idea of this sent me into a full panic attack. On some levels, it still does. I thought, "You want me to have my idea so clear that I can explain what it is and why someone should buy it/invest in it, in two minutes?" When it comes to your book's pitch, I have news: you need to be able to do it in thirty seconds. Preferably twenty.

If your hook is any longer than that, you're including unnecessary information, and/or you aren't clear enough on what your book is about, who it's for, and how it benefits them. Not to worry—there is a way through this insanity! Remember Marie Forleo's core message? Everything Is Figureoutable.

Oftentimes, we make the hook longer than it needs to be because we include information that is, in reality, only important to us. We fear leaving it out, because what if that little piece of info is the one piece the reader needs to hear in order to shout, "Oh! I need that!" In all honesty, when we do that, we're really only projecting our own fear that if we leave that little thing out, it didn't happen or we're suggesting that it isn't important. We need people to know that it happened. And that it was important. But once you realize you're doing this and why, you can quickly pivot.

I worked with an author whom I adore and who has been a rule follower since she entered this world. As such, she mercilessly wrestled with her hook for two days before ultimately saying, "I cannot get this any more succinct. Here's where I am: 'This book is about a mother's journey with infant loss, pre-term labor, a pre-term birth, a love of music, and a parent's illness. It's for anyone who wants to feel less alone, more inspired and hopeful, and who loves the mother/daughter bond. Also, music. Especially Stevie Nicks.'"

Because I know her well, I knew why each of these

moments in time was important to her (and would be to anyone who had experienced them). I knew how critical it was to her to include them in the book's content. And I reassured her that she absolutely could do that. Ironically, the reason she was including so many points of her own story and so many benefits to the reader was one and the same: she didn't want anyone to feel left out. But by including so many varied stories and benefits in her hook, she would, with absolutely zero intention, actually leave most people out. They'd be confused enough as to the main focus of the book and how it related to something they were either experiencing or curious about that their brains would say, "I don't get it," not "Oh, I need that."

Once she could relax a bit about the fact that she didn't need to get a gold star affixed to the top of the page on which she'd written her hook, and that she didn't need to have every story she wanted to tell, character she wanted to include, and song she'd ever loved included in her hook, the outline began to take shape, and the writing began to flow.

It's important to note that the hook is often more tightly honed *while* you're writing the book. The core message has to be established before you begin outlining, but a mistake many make is assuming they have to have their hook on point before they start outlining (or writing). That's not the case. So many of the details and nuances come to the surface *during* the writing. It's like Penney Peirce said in the introduction to her incredible book, *Frequency: The Power of Personal Vibration*, "Writing this book has been an education in itself for me. I thought I knew about vibration and sensitivity when I began, but the information and insights that spontaneously came to me in the process of writing were often mind-blowing."

When it comes to transformative nonfiction, the hook doesn't have to include detailed information that diagnoses the reasons your reader hasn't reached their goal. But in order to be most effective, it does need to speak to your reader's primary objections or incite intrigue, and it does need to speak to your reader's aspirational identity (who your reader aspires to become or a quality he or she aspires to have).

When editors in the traditional publishing world are deciding which books they'll acquire, there are five specific aspects of your hook that they consider.

First, your hook needs to be simple but powerful, and it needs to incite intrigue. "This book is about my experience going through loss" is simple, but it's not powerful, because it doesn't evoke curiosity. Make no mistake, your experience navigating loss is *no doubt* powerful. A prospective reader, however, needs to understand how your journey can, in some way, benefit them (and that benefit can be as simple as changing their perspective, helping them be more compassionate, or showing them a new way to look at life).

One way to incite intrigue is to combine common principles in a unique way. A great example of this is the subtitle of Mark Manson's bestseller, *The Subtle Art of Not Giving a F*ck*, which is: *How to Be Happier by Being Less Positive All the Time*. The prospective reader wants to be happier, so the hook has hit on his aspiration. But by suggesting that the way to do that is by being less positive, he's created intrigue by going against the more common directive that in order to be happier, we should simply see the good in absolutely everything.

To propose another example: Let's say you are someone who loves to travel but hates all the luggage that comes with it, so you've learned how to travel the world with just one suitcase. You're writing about how others can do the same (the premise being that you're teaching people how to travel luxuriously and often, but in a minimalistic way). That speaks to a reader's aspirations (traveling the world and minimalism), and it's also intriguing because we often think that traveling the world means figuring out how to accommodate four suitcases and two travel-ons per person. Does anyone else remember the movie "Sex and the City 2" where they went to Dubai? They had a lot of luggage. A luxurious vacation in Dubai? Yes, please. All that luggage? God, no.

Second, a powerful hook is clear in its benefits. To say, "My book will help you love more" or "It will help you have more motivation" is selling inspirationally. But it begs the question: How will your book do that? What is it going to do for or enable in your reader's life? Part of the book description for *The Monkey is the Messenger: Meditation and What Your Busy Mind is Trying to Tell You* by Ralph de la Rosa is: "Here at last—a remedy for all those who want to meditate but suppose they can't because they think too much." Just take my money already.

Third, the hook needs to be magnetic by speaking to your reader's exact challenge. This creates an attraction with your ideal reader that causes them to immediately think, "I need that. Now." This is what instantly sold me on *You Are A Badass* by Jen Sincero. The minute I perused the back cover and read what I considered to be the hook, I grabbed it without even reading the rest of the back cover copy! That hook? "You Are A Badass is the self-help book for people who desperately want to improve their lives but don't want to get busted doing it." I was sure I was on candid camera, but I felt so seen (figuratively) that I didn't even care.

Fourth, the hook must be niched. Remember, a book for everyone is for no one. If you're writing a book on how to find love, and you say your book is for every woman on the planet, that suggests that you're writing for a 20-year-old and an 80-year-old, which is going to be difficult, because those two age groups typically receive information quite differently. The language you'd use to speak to the 20-year-old would confuse not just the 80-year-old but also me, and I'm barely 50! Now, there is absolutely a chance that if you write for 30-somethings, an 80-year-old might be drawn to your book, but to write directly to a 20-year-old and an 80-year-old simultaneously is a difficult feat. A wonderful example of this is *When the F Will He Text: And How to Know If He's Worth the Wait* by Sara ONeil and Jacqueline Kravette. They wrote for twenty- and thirty-somethings, but the book's been well-received by women far older than that (including yours truly). Know *specifically* who you're writing for while remaining open to the idea that it may attract a far wider audience (hello, wildly unanticipated Harry Potter fans).

Fifth, a great hook is easily repeatable (shareable). This does not mean that people need to be able to memorize and repeat your hook on command. It means that if someone is reading your book on an airplane, feverishly underlining and proclaiming, "Yes! This!" to the point that their seatmate is compelled to ask what the book is about, you want the person who's now doing your promo for you (for free) to be able to easily communicate what the book is teaching them or helping them understand.

Sometimes, having a template to work off of is helpful when it comes to crafting your hook without overthinking. Yes, your hook will naturally become more succinct as you write, but having higher-level clarity on what your book is about, who it's for, and how the reader will benefit is incredibly helpful in making sure that your outline and writing stay on track.

A few of the hook templates I give my clients are:

- "My book explores a 4-step process to [what] for [target reader] who are experiencing [feeling] and want to be/feel [aspiration]." (transformative nonfiction)
- "I have created [process] to help [target reader] accomplish [specific goal] so they can [something they want] even if/without [common objection]." (transformative nonfiction)
- "This book details my journey through [core topic] so

[target reader] can finally [target reader's highest goal] without feeling [relatable emotion]." (inspirational memoir)

Once you've honed your hook—even if it doesn't fully come together until you're part-way (or all the way) through the writing—use the above five criteria to determine whether or not you can polish it even further to ensure that your target reader has no choice but to hit Buy Now.

CHAPTER 7

BECOME BFF WITH YOUR READER

N ow that you've gotten clear on your intention, defined your core message, and started clarifying your hook, it's time to consider your reader and how he or she will benefit from reading your book. Yes, I said reader. Singular. I'll explain why in a moment.

Once you know why and how you want to spread the word around your book's topic, you need to spend at least as much time (if not more) considering how your reader will benefit from the information you'll provide or the story you'll tell. These days more than ever, people's time and attention are spread thinner than my patience at the grocery store the day before Thanksgiving. So if you aren't clear about who will most benefit from your book and how, your reader won't be either. Which means they won't buy it!

The final aspect of your hook (which was discussed in the previous chapter) pertains to your reader, and people often leave that part blank (or somewhat nebulous) the first time around for three main reasons.

One, we so badly want our book to be for everyone. But think about it—if you're trying to write in a way that appeals to everyone, you're going to change your voice every third word. You're going to constantly wonder, "Should I swear? These guys like it if I swear." "Should I not swear? Those guys *hate* it when people swear." "Should I tell this story? People in this group may not understand what I'm talking about. And people in that group may be offended." All this does is create confusion about your unique voice and who you're designed to help, which only causes you to put the book back in the drawer for another few months.

I cannot tell you how many times I've heard, after a book was released, "I'm so confused. Every one of my Facebook friends said they'd buy my book. I have 4,978 Facebook friends, but I've only sold two copies." I'm rarely surprised, because beyond your mom and best friend, most people do not buy anything just to be of support, even if they say they will. Those who do often immediately put the book on the shelf, never even glancing at page one. This does exactly nothing for you as an author except put a few dollars in your bank account in the first month of sales.

Even if you have a huge friends-and-family support team who all purchase the book the day it comes out, your impact is likely going to be strongest *outside* that circle. Therefore, when the initial purchase run dies down after a week or so, you'll want to be incredibly confident about letting strangers know exactly what your book is about, who it's for, and how they'll benefit. That's what gets people placing their order while they're in the elevator with you. When someone knows they want something, they pull out their phone and order it, pronto. Otherwise, they say, "I'll take a look!" and they don't—either because they never had any intention to in the first place or because they legitimately forgot.

One of the most important things you can do at this and every stage of your journey as an author (and a human being) is recognize that your voice, style, and message simply are not for everyone. If it helps, remember that there are people out there who don't like JK Rowling. There are people who don't like Ellen DeGeneres. There are people who don't like Ryan Reynolds for God's sake. How is that possible? Not everyone will like you. And it's *not personal*. (We'll talk more about that in a bit.) But the people your voice is for? They'll love you forever and a day for making a connection with them in the way only you can.

The second reason people avoid the "reader" section of the hook template is that it feels painful and heavy and unfun. It does, for *everyone*. No author is having more fun with this than you are. There's not something wrong with you because you don't want to spend time getting clearer on who your target reader is. But I promise, while it may not feel like it right now, taking the time to do so is one of the "shortcuts" to a powerful book that performs the way you want it to (if not better).

The third argument for avoiding this task is that people (understandably) don't want to micro-analyze the brand of makeup their target reader prefers or which TikTok influencer they're presently obsessed with. I've worked with wonderful coaches and mentors over the years who were adamant that I create an ideal customer "avatar" for each of my products and programs. This delightful exercise often involved knowing what kind of pizza they liked and which magazines they preferred to read on the plane when they jetted off to wherever for the weekend. It was also important that I know where they were jetting off to when they did said jetting. In those coaches' defense, knowing your customer to this level when you're selling a product or service often creates the most direct path out of obscurity, but when it comes to your ideal reader, I recommend a slightly different process. Because assessing your target reader's favorite cheat meal or preference of manual over electronic toothbrush is a level to which you don't need to dive.

Doing a solid level of exploration into who your target reader is helps greatly; not doing so causes frequent moments when you're trying to write for (and please) too many people. As a result, you lose your voice as your ego declares, "You'll never sell a lot of books if you're only speaking to one person. Keep struggling to speak to the masses, Claire." Tell your ego to shut it down, because that is completely untrue, and Claire is going to be just fine. While counterintuitive, when you write for just *one* person, your book often has the greatest impact, because when all is said and done, we aren't all that different from one another. There are only so many desires and challenges, and nearly all of them fall into one of the following categories: health, wealth, personal development, or relationships.

Writing for one person works well for the same reason it works well to have an intimate conversation with one person. When you're having a one-on-one conversation with someone, you're likely just being yourself—especially when you feel comfortable with that person. That comfort comes across as exactly that. Not as pushy or demanding or convincing. You're being you, and the person you're talking to often says things like, "Yes! That's exactly how I feel!" or "Oh my gosh, I had to switch to decaf coffee recently too! So glad we're aging together!"

Another obvious but often-overlooked benefit of writing for one person is, you aren't focused on anyone else. You aren't thinking, "What if I start talking about my favorite meat dish and there's a vegan in the room?" You aren't worried about offending anyone. You aren't worried about trying to convince everyone. You aren't trying to prove yourself. You're simply being you, offering suggestions or guidance or thoughts in the name of love and service. And that's how true connection happens. It's just as easy to put that energy out to the masses as it is to put it toward one person, which is why people often propose killing as many birds with one stone as possible (a violent metaphor indeed). But as oxymoronic as it might seem, the way you most effectively speak to the masses is by speaking to one person. Because in truth, we're all one. So identify your target reader, and speak directly to him or her.

When I wrote my first book, now titled *Holy Sh*t...I'm*

Having Twins! I spoke to one person—a new mom of twins who was the primary caregiver and had a toddler at home as well. When I wrote *You Cannot Be Serious: and 32 Other Rules that Sustain a (Mostly) Balanced Mom*, I spoke to a woman who's a mom and is also pursuing her dreams as a business owner or a businesswoman. When I wrote *Enough*, I spoke to a mom who's running ragged trying to do it all, have it all, and be it all, and has lost herself along the way.

Knowing your target reader's challenges and aspirations is far more important when writing transformative nonfiction than it is when writing memoir. When writing memoir, it's more impactful to identify the books your target reader has already enjoyed, because the journey, style, insights, or perspectives are similar. Consider the template: If you liked [insert book title], you'll love my book. For example, readers who liked *Love Warrior* by Glennon Doyle will also likely enjoy *Tiny Beautiful Things* by Cheryl Strayed or *Buy Yourself the Fucking Lilies* by Tara Schuster. You can do this exercise with transformative nonfiction as well, and it's a great way to market your book via social media graphics. (If you liked [insert other book cover], you'll love [insert your book cover]).

Let's move on to how to identify your target (or ideal) reader without losing time analyzing preferences that make little to no difference in the grand scheme of things. In the coaching space, the term "ideal client" has been floating around for years. Since I anticipate that many reading this book either are coaches or would like to be, it's a good parallel to draw as we go deeper into how to identify your ideal reader. Coaches are often asked to describe their ideal client in terms of the challenges they have, how they think about those challenges and their ability to solve them, how much disposable income they have, their education level, and whether they prefer red or green M&Ms.

Honestly, intentions are good, but going through this process with the wrong perspective dehumanizes the people you're trying to understand more than it helps you help them. It takes them from a warm-blooded person with a challenge to a roboticized player you are trying to control. Simone Seol (who is a mind-blowingly brilliant coach; look her up) recently expressed the boiled-down version of "ideal client" beautifully in an Instagram post (and I'm paraphrasing): It's someone who you love working with and who loves working with you. It's truly that simple. When considering your ideal reader, you don't have to think any differently. Your ideal reader is someone who has a challenge you can solve; who loves your style; and who you love connecting with, getting to know, and guiding. If you can identify one person who fits that bill, I can promise you that there are at least 1,000 more (if not 100,000 more) who will identify with your target reader's challenge and like your style enough to invest in your book.

Some of the aspects frequently used to describe an ideal client (or reader) are neither productive nor fair. It's not effective to define your target reader based on whether she is someone you can control when it comes to how fast she implements your proposed solutions. It's not someone who's likely to get results in 6.2 minutes so they can write a glowing testimonial that gets you more clients. It's not someone who has so much money that they can pay you over and over and over again until the end of time. All those things may be true, but they do not, in and of themselves, constitute an ideal reader.

Every human being goes through a similar series of events when it comes to an unsolved—and perhaps perceived to be unsolvable—challenge.

To illustrate my approach to getting to know your ideal reader, let's explore a challenge that I know you're intimately familiar with: wanting to write a book but not being sure where to start. The way people who experience this challenge navigate this series of events helps clarify why one person ends up churning out a book every year, while others let those years pass, starting each new one saying, "This is the year I'm going to get this book written!" but never making good on that declaration.

In Shakespeare's *Hamlet*, Hamlet says, "Why, then, 'tis none to you, for there is nothing either good or bad, but thinking makes it so." That aforementioned series of events every human being goes through? It's so well-studied that it serves as the basis for a common coaching technique, referred to as CTFAR (which stands for Circumstance, Thought, Feeling, Action, Result). According to most spiritual and philosophic traditions, everything that happens to a person in his or her life, every circumstance, is, at its core, a neutral event. It's neither good nor bad, happy nor sad, right nor wrong. It's just a "thing" that happens or an idea that you have—until you have a thought about it that makes it good or bad, happy or sad, right or wrong. First, therefore, we have to start with the triggering (and neutral) event. Your target reader's circumstance is, in itself, a neutral event. *Your* circumstance, and the reason you're reading this book (you want to write a powerful book of your own), is also a neutral event.

The issue starts to boil up when someone has a thought about that (neutral) event, almost immediately after it presents itself. When it comes to writing a book, the thought that quickly arises fits into one of two categories. Category One: "I have no idea where this is going, but let's start outlining!" or "I have no idea how to do this, but I'm committed to figuring it out." Category Two: "Who am I to think I can do something like that?" or "I wish I had the skills to write a great book, but I don't think I do."

The thought then creates a feeling/emotion. When talking about a challenge someone has tried multiple times to overcome without success, the person has thoughts we could label as "negative." For example: "I'm not good enough" or "I'm not unique. My message isn't that special." As a result, he continues to put off the task of writing his book.

When a thought is repeated over and over again, it becomes a belief. That feeling that starts with "I can't" or "I shouldn't" or "I won't" or "I'll never" eventually morphs into a belief. Now you don't just feel it; you *believe* it. Feelings aren't facts, but beliefs are far more readily seen by the ego as factual. And once a feeling becomes a belief, it affects the action a person takes (or doesn't take). If you believe that you're never going to figure out how to start writing the book, you continue to procrastinate, slowly giving up. You think, "Why bother?" and rake the leaves in the backyard or watch another season of "Billions" instead of taking ten minutes to consider your book's core message. And that action leads to the result, which is that nothing changes, and the book doesn't get written.

This is where your reader's greatest sadness lies. Because they *want* change. In this example, they *want* to write the book. They just have no idea how to get there, and everything they've tried so far has failed.

If you substitute your target reader's challenge into this equation, what do they want? What do they think when it comes to getting it? What beliefs have that thought, on repeat, formed? And what result is that creating in their life in this particular area? *That* is what you need to get clear about when it comes to who your target reader is, not their favorite flavor of bubblegum. It's *not* about manipulation. Ever. It's about understanding and, when called for, compassion.

If the initial thought one has in response to an idea or a desire is, "I've got this!" and that thought creates feelings of excitement and empowerment and faith, the belief would become, "I'll just keep figuring it out, step by step!" That person may still need your book, by the way, because they don't know what that step-by-step process is, or they want to build upon the process they already have in place. Speaking to them is easier because all you have to know is that they want to write a book (for example), and you can show them a process for doing that. But some of your greatest impact will come from letting those who are haggling with the limiting thoughts that keep so many of us from pursuing what we really want know that you get it, and you can help if they're willing to put a bit of trust in you. The first step is showing them that you truly understand what they want, why they're so frustrated, and how you can help them in a way that's different from what they've tried so far.

By understanding this process, I can get to the essence of who my ideal reader is, and I can speak to him or her in a way that deeply resonates. With that in mind, let's talk about some of the most potent questions to ask yourself about your ideal reader in order to get completely clear on who they are so you can speak directly to them:

- What does my ideal reader want when it comes to the topic I'm discussing?
- What is my ideal reader's biggest challenge when it comes to this topic?
- How does my ideal reader feel about this challenge? How does the challenge express itself in my ideal reader's thoughts?
- How do these thoughts make my ideal reader feel?
- What is the story my ideal reader is telling herself based on the feelings he or she has about this challenge? In other words, what are the beliefs my ideal reader has developed when it comes to solving this challenge?

The biggest secret I have for getting in sync with your ideal reader? Write her a letter. You can even give your target reader a name if you'd like. Begin with *Dear Bridget* (or whatever name you've chosen). Then, let her know that you know what she's going through. Elaborate so she can trust that you truly understand. Remind her that you know how she feels (again, by clarifying the thoughts and feelings you know she's having). Reassure her that things can be different, and communicate how you know this to be true. Let her know exactly how you're going to walk her toward her goals.

For the record, yes, it's completely normal to feel like the letter you're writing is to a previous version of *you*. That happens more often than not. Because the reason you know this person so intimately is that you were him or her! And because you're now in a different space, you know you are the perfect person to help them take that next step (or steps) toward a different reality.

CHAPTER 8

CREATE AN EPIC OUTLINE

There are people who love the process of outlining, and there are people who hate it. In the literary world, authors often self-characterize as "plotters" or "pantsers." Plotters work off a pre-determined book structure, while pantsers are so named because they fly by the seat of their pants, letting the story take them wherever it does. Neither approach is right or wrong. I'm both a plotter and a pantser. But I most definitely start with a structure and then allow my creativity to fill in the gaps. Without a basic structure to follow, the blank page would send me running for the latest Netflix craze every time.

Typically, people who love outlining feel that way because they love structure. People who dislike it do so because structure makes them feel restricted. They want to write from a "place of inspiration," which is poetic in theory but often unproductive in practice.

Think of the outline from the perspective of an architect. When building a house, if tradesmen just show up with a bunch of wood and some concrete, there are few architects on earth who will have the vision to pour the foundation and put the two-by-fours in the right place to ensure that all the rooms end up being the right size and in the right place (with none being left out). Book outlines are important for the exact same reason. Regardless of when you outline—whether you do it first thing or after writing the first draft—an outline is a necessary component. If you don't outline early on, you'll want to reverse outline when your first draft is complete. Reverse outlining is the process whereby you create an outline retroactively based on what you've written. It allows you to ensure that your content flows well, isn't repetitive, hasn't left out critical information, and doesn't pose issues when it comes to the order in which you're delivering information.

Because it's a common question, I'll note that, occasionally, repeating content is valuable when a point deserves to be made again for emphasis. But when it's unintentional and the repetition is occurring because the author doesn't remember that she already told the story or made the point, it's gratuitous and confusing to the reader. Returning to the house-building analogy, you can decide at the last minute that you don't need the formal dining room or mancave you forgot to plan for, but the same can't be said for a bathroom or kitchen sink. Laying out a house ad hoc while building it is no doubt a creative endeavor, but it often leads to a situation where you have to break apart the family room because you're left with only enough space to have a five-square-foot kitchen.

If you're more creative and go-with-the-flow, you certainly *can* write without outlining (if you choose) and fill in gaps later on. But for most people, having a basic understanding of what each chapter's main point is and what stories best support that main point helps the writing flow with far greater ease. Having an outline allows your writing sessions to be focused and intentional. Sitting down for your ten or thirty minutes of writing time and wondering, "What do I write about today?" isn't terribly productive. It causes people to either waste time or end up talking about something they've already talked about (twice). An outline, on the other hand, allows you to easily pick up exactly where you left off.

The reason most people who resist the outline do so is, ironically, the same reason they need it. The thought that you need to get *all* of your content ideas or topics out of your head and onto the page (even in outline form) usually feels quite overwhelming. So people tell themselves the story that "I'm a person who likes to write from wherever my soul wants to speak from each day." That process is not "wrong," but when you're finished and go back and create the outline retroactively, you might very well find that you talked about the same thing multiple times and never once addressed some of the topics you really wanted to cover (and now aren't sure where they fit in). It creates a different—but equally unnecessary—level of overwhelm, which, ironically, the writer was trying to avoid in the first place by not creating the outline!

Remember that the outline is meant to be fluid. It's intended to support flow and creativity, not stifle it. It allows you to be creative within confined boundaries. Also, you aren't mandated to commit to it in its entirety. Again using the house-building analogy, if you plan for the family room to be in the front of the house, but later on decide you'd like it in the back, most custom builders will find a way to allow you to make that shift. If you don't plan for it at all, however, it can be hard to figure out how to incorporate it without increasing the footprint of the entire home, which is both costly and time-consuming.

You can combine chapters later on if one doesn't end up having enough depth on its own. You can also separate what you initially thought would only be one chapter into two (or even three) if it becomes clear that doing so would make the content more digestible for the reader. I also suggest that authors create a Topic Idea/Story Parking Lot where they put stories and thoughts that come to them randomly and cause them to think, "Maybe this should go in the book, but I'm not sure." When these topic ideas/stories come to you, do not insist that you'll remember them later! You won't, so write them down when you think of them. One might work in the book, and one might work better in a post or on a podcast. All content is valuable *somewhere*, but it doesn't necessarily belong in the book you're currently writing!

You may be wondering, "What exactly defines a chapter?" A chapter is a single cohesive idea or thought, often in the chronological order of your journey (memoir) or one of your teachings, lessons, guideposts, or steps in your process, where each step typically builds upon the one before (nonfiction).

In order to create your outline's basic structure, consider eight to ten topics you know you want to address. (If this already feels like too much, start with three to five.) For now, you can consider each of these to be chapters, even though they may not end up being standalone chapters in the final book.

Once you identify eight to ten topics you want to discuss, determine whether each of those topics can inspire an entire chapter's worth of content by asking yourself, "Is this a standalone topic?" In other words, "Could I talk about this topic alone on a stage for five minutes?" Then ask yourself, "Why does my reader need to know this?" The latter question is most helpful when writing material that's highly emotional. Sometimes you'll think you want to write an entire chapter on a particular topic, but when you ask yourself, "Why does the reader need to know this?" the answer you don't want to have is, "because I want the reader to 'side' with me and come to the conclusion that I was right, and my ex is indeed an asshole." You are writing to guide your reader, not hoping that the reader will validate you! When that's the case—if, for example, you still have anger toward someone else that needs to be released—your soul may need to have its own cathartic experience by getting emotions out of your body and onto paper. That's perfectly fine. Just remember to clean it up later!

When outlining memoir, start with what your life looked like *before* the challenge presented itself. From there, you can engage in the outline creation process using the Hero's Journey as your framework. One of the best books I've found detailing the Hero's Journey framework for writers is *Super Structure* by James Scott Bell. This framework doesn't work as well, in my experience, for transformative nonfiction, so don't feel the need to conform to it if that's the genre you're writing. An understanding of it might, however, help you to craft stories that keep the reader reading, as it's a proven storytelling framework, which is why it's followed for most bestselling novels and blockbuster movies.

My full-fledged book outlining process is a bit too detailed to cover in its entirety in this book, but you can get instant access to the Book Outlines Made Simple workshop available on my website. In this workshop, I first walk you through the anatomy of a bestselling book, clarifying the five critical components of books that sell again and again while attracting amazing readers and possibly even new clients who are excited to work with and learn from you. We then clarify your core message in order to remove all confusion around what topics to cover and which stories to tell, as well as identify how to ensure that your target readers say, "This book is *exactly* what I need!" And finally, I reveal my exact outline formula so you can create an epic book skeleton that helps you masterfully organize your thoughts, experiences, and insights into a powerful book readers can't put down. You can access the workshop at PublishAProfitableBook.com/bookoutline.

CHAPTER 9

WRITE THE DAMN BOOK ALREADY

I t's time. I trust that you've at least *started* your outline, so now we're going to start writing. I may have just heard a few of you mumble, "Oh God," but stay with me. Because I know what your brain is likely doing right now, let me remind you that the thought you have that this is hard for you but not for anyone else is just...wrong. Writing a book is hard. Period. The first draft of every book ever written is shit. But it gives you something to work with. To hone. To mold. No one sits down and whips out a perfect first draft. By the time you read a book you fall in love with, it's been edited many, many times.

I remember when Annabel Monaghan joined me on the Write the Damn Book Already podcast to talk about writing *Nora Goes Off Script*. She stated that her first official draft was 100 pages (it's women's fiction, and the published book is 272 pages in length). Her trusted editing team said, and

I'm paraphrasing, "This is not a book. Yet." But she had something to work with, to build upon, to expand. And the final product? It's so good. Just go buy a copy already, and happy weekend to you!

I was recently asked, "What is the bridge between the outline and the writing?" As in, "How do I know when I've outlined *enough* to dive in and start writing?" The answer is different for everyone, which I realize may, once again, not be the exact answer you were looking for. But in fact, it's the answer you want, because it helps to validate that whatever works for you in this area is perfect.

Some people need only the most basic outline with simple main topics. From there, they can easily sit down and bring forth everything they want to say on each of those topics. Other people need extremely detailed outlines, the kind we used to create in high school English Lit or History class, that had more levels than Super Mario Bros. And some people fall somewhere in between. Some need to outline in great detail when it comes to one particular chapter and in far less detail for another because it's a topic about which they speak so often that the outline lives in the forefront of their mind and easily teleports to the page. No level of detail when it comes to the outline is inherently better than another. What it comes down to is how much of the content you need to flesh out in order to sit down and write without wondering what on earth you ever thought you'd say on a particular subject matter.

No matter how many times I remind people, it's easy to forget that none of the books we love so much that we recommend them like crazy—or have them sitting in a "to-be-read…again" pile—were written by people who sat down, whipped out chapter 3, sent it to their editor, and got a note back that said, "Holy shit. I've literally never said this to an author before, but I don't have a single suggestion. It's simply…perfect. You're a unicorn." The number of rounds of edits each chapter (let alone an entire book) goes through in order to get from "This is how the material initially flowed out of me" to "This is actually comprehensible" would blow most people's minds. The collaboration between editor and author in that regard is incredibly intimate, and it's why great trust is required between the two in order to polish the finished product to a high shine.

Sometimes (which is the understatement of the century), a first-time author concludes that she's the only one who can't write a perfect chapter on the first try, is clearly doing something horrifically wrong, and is being sent a clear and present message by the universe to cease and desist immediately, if not sooner. When this happens, there's an analogy I enjoy presenting for consideration. It involves the symphony (or, if you prefer, a Broadway musical).

When classical music lovers attend the symphony, they don their finest frocks and gracefully glide toward their velvet-covered seats, anxiously anticipating an evening of jaw-dropping musical entertainment. They can hear the musicians warming up from behind the curtain, and then the lights dim, everyone takes their seats, audience chatter dissipates, and the curtain opens. There they sit, practiced musicians with pristine posture in coordinated ensembles, instruments resting uniformly on their laps or the floor in front of them. The conductor walks on stage, equally decked out in his (or her) opening night attire, raises the baton, and in an instant the audience is transfixed, remaining that way for the rest of the show.

But do you honestly think this is what it looked like on Day 1 of rehearsals? Because I can assure you, it did not. The musicians, who are all professionals and masters of their crafts, and who have been practicing said crafts for years if not decades, showed up in jeans, shorts, a Boston Celtics T-shirt, and possibly parachute pants circa 1983. The conductor can possibly only be singled out because he (or she) is the one walking around holding the baton. The baton is raised, the musicians begin playing the music they've been practicing on their own for months, and within four measures, the conductor is yelling, "Cut!"

They then spend the rest of that rehearsal (and all of those that follow) honing, re-working, and otherwise practicing playing, both as individuals and as a collective, until the conductor determines they are ready to play in front of an audience without any season ticket holders asking for a refund. Each of the musicians likely has a portion of the music he has to practice a bit more thoroughly. Again, *these are professionals who are the best of the best at their craft*, who often still have to audition for their spot on the stage. They absolutely do not get it perfect—or anywhere close—on the first try.

I proposed this analogy to one of my authors who was having a hard time accepting that even the best of the best's books start out a little shaky, and their editor ultimately plays a huge role in getting those books from great concepts not perfectly expressed on paper to solid, un-put-downable books.

She asked, "So, in this scenario, is the book editor the conductor?" A brilliant question. In the orchestra world, the conductor has the final say when it comes to which section needs to be played more loudly, or which needs to slow down, or which measures need to be canceled altogether. In the book world, the editor has the final say (when one is being traditionally published). But if you're an author who is independently published or self-published, *you* have the final say. It's your creation. And that can be scary, because of course we want someone else to direct us, saying, "Do it this way. Put this here and this there. Don't say this; say far more about that."

That kind of direction would allow us to let ourselves off the hook by blaming the editor if someone didn't like the end product. But I promise, taking ownership of your creation is so much more powerful in the long term. Every great creative in history has ultimately had to take responsibility for his or her unique creation. Can you imagine if someone had said to Picasso, "These drawings are just too simple. Make them more ornate" and he'd listened? Or if someone had said to Monet, "The lilies don't work for me. Take out the lilies and people will love your work." Or if someone had said to Usher, "The first eight notes of 'Yeah' just aren't that catchy. Ditch 'em." I mean, I shudder. Yes, you'll need to trust your editor a hell of a lot. And when it's time to put the final polish on it before the curtain opens, you'll have to trust yourself most of all.

Keeping with this analogy for just a moment longer, there will be times when you're writing and think, "I don't feel like I know this material or my process or how I feel about the difference between dahlias and daisies as well as I thought I did." Perhaps you'll think, "I don't know if I've fully processed this part of my story well enough to write about it honestly and eloquently." When this happens, consider the musician who is on his first run-through of the music, gets to page fourteen, measure eleven, and thinks, "This part is not easy to play this fast!" What would happen if he then said, "I bet I'm the only one having trouble with this music. I'm clearly not meant to be a part of this symphony. I'll quit tomorrow." I'll tell you what would happen: the orchestra would go from 100 musicians to zero overnight.

Most professional musicians know that there will be at least one part of the music that will be harder than another (and that won't be as hard for another musician, even one who plays the same instrument). You know what they commit to doing? Practicing that part. Over and over again. I know this because one of my closest friends is a professional musician, and this is exactly what he does. It's an opportunity to get better, to gain more confidence, to become a stronger performer.

When you come upon a piece of your story or message that you don't feel capable of speaking to as strongly as you initially thought, see it as an opportunity to grow in your knowledge, your self-awareness, and your ability to serve

someone else at a higher level. Your increased clarity benefits not only you but everyone your message touches. When
people ask you about that aspect of your story or message,
you won't stumble. In fact, you'll be incredibly excited by
the question, given your newfound deeper understanding
of your perspective.

The *only* difference between you and the authors whose
books you read and become obsessed with is that they
made a decision not to let the challenges stop them. They
made a decision to grow through the challenges and to allow those challenges to make them better, stronger people.

When it comes down to the nitty-gritty of "So...do I just
sit down and write?" one of the first questions you likely
have is: "How often do I have to write, and for how long?
Because I'm very busy!" I know. I am too. I have five kids. I
wrote my first, second, and third books when up to four of
those kids were under the age of six. At one point in this
journey, I also had three completely untrained dogs. Additionally, I love (and I mean love) Netflix. And sleep. So if I
can get my books written, you can get yours written. I'm
sure of it.

Everyone has a different approach when it comes to a
writing schedule. Some people wake up at 5am (I am not
one of those people; positively nothing that I produce before 9am is comprehensible). Some people carve out an
hour a day, every other day. Some people schedule thirty
minutes a day, three days per week. There is truly no right
or wrong way—unless the way you choose isn't working on
a consistent basis.

It's been argued that if you don't write every day, you won't get your book written in a reasonable period of time. However, I've found that the most important variable when it comes to getting your book written isn't that you commit to a specific writing schedule but that you know yourself well enough to know what will work for you in order to set up a writing practice that's sustainable. After all, if you're someone who can dive into something head-first and be committed for seven days, but then you fall off the wagon never to return, this approach isn't terribly helpful after those first seven days—much like New Year's resolutions for the vast majority of us.

I advise my clients to pencil in twenty to thirty minutes a day, six days a week, but they're often working with me in a twelve-week program, and their goal is to get their rough first draft written in twelve weeks. This is absolutely doable, provided that every time you sit down for those twenty to thirty minutes, you know exactly what you're going to write about so that every word counts. It's precisely how I wrote the book you're presently reading! And I know you can carve out twenty minutes a day. It may mean giving up something else for a short time, but remember that it's only for a short time, not forever. Also, keep in mind the end you're working toward and how it will feel when you're finished. That's often a huge motivator—if you never finish, you'll be imagining the finish line for years, and there is little that is less motivating than that!

If twenty minutes per day, six days per week feels heavy, schedule twenty minutes three times a week. Or an hour twice a week. Or two hours every Saturday. But schedule something. Without getting into a routine and sticking to it, the timeline will simply get drawn out. This is true for any goal!

I used to advise that people aim for 50,000 words and then divide that by the length of time they wanted to take to write the book in order to determine how many words to shoot for each time they sat down to write. But all words are not valuable. I could type "I'm lost" over and over again for 2,000 words, but that's not the same as writing 2,000 valuable words! So just sit down and let the words flow out of you for your allotted time period.

Another question you'd probably like answered before you start writing is, "How long does this thing have to be?" A book shouldn't be long just for the sake of being long. Yes, there are indeed people who enjoy reading short books. But that fact shouldn't be the basis for arguing the merits of writing a 20,000-word book. After all, if we're going to present that fact as justification for penning a short book, we also have to consider a reader's motivation for preferring such short books. If someone commits to reading one book per week for a year, they are likely choosing shorter books for no other reason than they can't read a 300-page book every week for an entire year!

There are many 50,000-word books that are full of value. There are also 75,000-word books that simply repeat the same point over and over again (the goal was seemingly to hit a specific word count, not provide value over the full spectrum of its pages). By the same token, there are shorter books that are incredibly impactful—*The Alchemist* by Paulo Coelho, *We Should All Be Feminists* by Chimamanda Ngozi Adichie, and *Man's Search for Meaning* by Viktor Frankl among them.

There's no magic number when it comes to how many words your book should have. Same goes for number of chapters. Most nonfiction books average between twelve and eighteen chapters, but that doesn't mean that you can't have ten. Or thirty-two! When we focus too heavily on word or chapter count, we ignore what's most important, which is providing a valuable experience for the reader.

People also often overthink which software to use for writing, and the short answer is: it doesn't matter. Just pick one! I write in Microsoft Word. I have clients who write in Scrivener or Google Docs or Pages or on paper (yes, for real). If you are someone who loves writing with pen and paper, I do advise that once you're a few weeks in, you transfer all of your writing to a computer, because it's otherwise going to feel quite overwhelming once you finish and have 60,000 words to type!

Write without any sense of perfectionism, and whatever you do, do not edit as you go! This only takes up valuable time that could be spent getting the content out of your head. Trust me, you'll have ample time when all of the content has been written to go back and hone it. Many times, thinking, "I'll start the next chapter after I've perfected this one" is merely a form of procrastination because something about the next chapter feels daunting. Or, you're starting to question yourself a bit when it comes to writing at all, and you're going back through previously written content almost to prove to yourself that you *shouldn't* be writing the book. This is incredibly common, so if you find yourself doing it, know that you're completely normal, and also that you need to move on to the next chapter!

CHAPTER 10

A FEW WORDS ON IMPACTFUL CONNECTION

One of the reasons books are such an incredible resource is that they allow us to deeply connect with another human being—one who might live thousands of miles away and whom we otherwise wouldn't be able to meet—in a way that's incredibly personal. Almost as personal as if we were sitting right next to them. In fact, as an author, I've received no greater compliment than "As I read your book, it felt like you were sitting in my living room, talking right to me."

There are two aspects of creating this intense level of connection through nonfiction specifically that I refer to as Powerful Vulnerability™ and Compelling Compassion™.

POWERFUL VULNERABILITY™

Powerful Vulnerability refers to the art and science of sharing your less-than-glowing stories—the ones you're embarrassed to share or that you worry might make you appear "weak"—in a way that causes your readers to respect you even more than they did before. It's about sharing your hard, this-actually-happened moments (in other words, being vulnerable) in an authentic, powerful way. It's about sharing your struggle—*without* inviting people to feel bad for you and tell me how great you are because that's what you're *really* after.

The ability to be Powerfully Vulnerable is where we most clearly see the difference between writing about something you've actually experienced and writing about something simply because you think it will sell. There are a lot of "coaches" and "experts" and "gurus" who teach people to go to Amazon and research highly searched phrases, then write a book on that topic. The idea behind this approach is that if it's a highly searched phrase, it's also a topic that people have a lot of interest in. So if you write a book on that topic, you can conceivably sell it to a lot of people.

The challenge arises when the highly searched phrase is "anxiety recovery" and you've only experienced anxiety once (maybe). You cannot authentically write a book about that, which is why I don't subscribe to that approach. I realize that some people say they've done well by it, but it doesn't make sense to me. I'm passionate about people writing from where they've been and what they've experienced. Because more often than not, people who think, "Nobody cares about my story; I'm just little old me" will be amazed by how many people *will* care about their story. Because people want to read about normal, regular, everyday people who have gone through something similar to what they're going through and have figured out solutions they can employ in their own life.

Learning from somebody like Oprah or the Dalai Lama about the way they solve problems is valuable, yes. But it's also easy to fall back on the fact that Oprah has a massive house and a staff of seventy-seven. (To be clear, I have no idea how big her staff is.) My point is that it's easy to say, "Of course that person was able to handle it because they had the huge support team or the nice outfits or the right contacts or the big trust fund." But when you find a regular, everyday person who could quite easily be living next door (which is precisely where the phrase "girl next door" is conceptually based), their approach feels more accessible and doable. It's easier to believe "If they can do it, I can do it," and that's where the power, the magic, and the impact lie.

In order to have this level of impact, however, it's critical that you heal your wounds or process your grief enough that you can speak to incredibly painful moments or experiences in your life without doing so in a way that makes readers feel like they need to give *you* a hug because it's clear that you desperately need one! It's about sharing in a way that doesn't ask for confirmation or validation that you are right and another person is wrong. It's about sharing from a place of "This sucked. But I got through it and I'm stronger now, so I'm here to show you how you can get there too." This is what the "powerful" aspect of Powerful Vulnerability is all about.

Remember, your readers see you as the guide. They

absolutely want to know that you are human, which is why vulnerability is so important. But if they find themselves wanting to coach or comfort *you*, you haven't exhibited the powerful component of Powerful Vulnerability.

Writing about another's role in your journey is rarely easy, especially when their behavior wasn't exactly a shining moment. This is why, when you're first writing, you may find that a great deal of anger, resentment, or blame comes out. It will feel powerful, no doubt, but not in an *em*powering way. It will quickly become clear that there's no way you can publish a lot of what you're writing, because jail is not where most of us are looking to spend our summers. As a result, you may wonder whether writing this particular content is "worth it" or whether you should put the whole thing on hold until you can write about it without wanting to put your fist through the drywall.

If and when that happens (and it happens more often than you may think), I encourage you to keep on writing—not because the material will stay in the book, but because it very clearly needs to be expressed. Once you've done that, you clean it up to the point where you are back in the powerful position of guiding.

To that end, there are several suggestions I have to offer when it comes to writing about others' not-so-glowing role in your journey. No one wants to be sued for libel, and this is the primary concern people have when they are writing about someone else—especially if that someone else can be easily identified even without mentioning their name, because they're readily identifiable based on their role in your experience.

As I mentioned in Objection #8, you have every right to your perception of an experience. You do not, however, have a right to the other person's perception. There are often three sides to every story: yours, theirs, and the truth. Speaking about how you felt is something you have every right to do. But speaking to someone else's character through labeling (narcissist, selfish asshole, etc.) is not only a recipe for trouble, but it also weakens your credibility. The minute you start to sound angry or bitter, it becomes clear that perhaps you aren't quite ready to be publicly speaking on the topic.

If people are going to hire you to speak to their group or organization, they want to be confident that you can maintain a professional demeanor throughout. If you can't do that in the controlled environment of a book, the possibility that you'll lose your cool on stage is perhaps a bit too high for comfort. In short, focus on telling *your* story. Starting to tell someone else's story, making assumptions, labeling others, or in any way trying to position yourself as "right" are indicators that you're crossing into dangerous territory. The goal should never be to throw someone else under the bus; the goal is to powerfully share your experience.

A key point when it comes to vulnerability in book writing (not to mention life in general): you do not owe anyone any more detail on a topic or experience than you are comfortable providing at any given point in time. Just because something happened in your life and you are writing a book does not require that you divulge information or details that you purposely choose to keep private for one reason or another. Many times, people fear that if they don't address every possible question or tell every single story, if they aren't willing to talk about *all* of it, they're being disingenuous. They're not. What they're doing is having boundaries. Boundaries will save you. I encourage you in creating them, and I support you in upholding them!

One of the most brilliant executors of Powerful Vulnerability I've seen is Jen Hatmaker. While on tour to promote her newest book, *Feed These People: Slam-Dunk Recipes for Your Crew*, she stands on stage in front of thousands and acknowledges that she got divorced, that she wasn't an active participant in the decision, and that it was an extremely difficult time for her. But that's where the details end. She takes you right up to the edge of the "drama" but not into it. From that point, she focuses on how she looks at and works through the challenges she encounters in life, which is *exactly* what her audience wants to hear.

Sure, there are the random few wackadoos who want all the gory details and are quick to do less-than-classy Google searches on the matter. There are the random few who will criticize her for not giving away more information than she does, suggesting that she "owes" her fans an accounting of her every personal detail. But she's as beloved as she is precisely because she took the time to do the work to figure out how *she* felt first. She stands in her power, holding her boundaries. And in so doing, she teaches others to do the same. She shows her audience what it looks like to love both herself *and* her people, fiercely. She found her own light first and then focused on shining that light out-ward. What she didn't (and doesn't) do is invite oth-ers—subtly or not-so-subtly—to help her *find* her light.

Choose what you're willing and ready to be vulnerable about. Put firm boundaries around it. Share it powerfully. And before long, you'll transition from leading yourself to leading an entire flock.

COMPELLING COMPASSION™

Compelling Compassion is a concept by which you move the reader to take action *without* shaming him or her. It's about compelling them to make a shift while having com-passion for where they are and the hardships that keep them stuck.

If you're like me, directives like "Just do it" or "If you really wanted things to be different, you'd make the changes already" don't work. And there is a reason. At their core, they're said for the benefit of the person who's saying them, not the receiver. The person saying them wants (if not needs) the receiver to make changes on *their* timeline, perhaps because they're looking to prove the value of *their* advice/guidance. In other words, they're looking to feed their own ego or bank account. Alternatively, perhaps they are out of suggestions and simply don't want to talk about it with you any further. Neither provides a strong argument for you to run off and "just do it," regardless of what Nike might have to say about that.

The most helpful guidance often comes in the form of compassionate ass-kicking (which is what Compelling

Compassion is, at its core). It's about not being willing to support the idea of someone staying where they are by continuing to support their reasons for doing so (often referred to as excuses) while having compassion for the fact that change is often hard. It's hard because it's multi-layered and based in patterns that have been in place for a long time. It's therefore important to give people strategies and help them see the possibilities in terms of what's *really* keeping them stuck, but do so in a way that also acknowledges that the person isn't broken, and you aren't there to fix them (and certainly not on your timetable; that kind of pressure never helps, and it often hurts).

When I coach people who are writing a book, I believe, in the depths of my soul, in their message and their ability to share that message in the form of a book. And I know, in the depths of my soul, that they might get it done in twelve weeks. Or it might take two years. I *also* know that if it takes two years, the book that ends up being written will be so much more potent than the one that would have been written in twelve weeks simply because I forced them to adhere to my timeline so I could tell the world, "I help people write books in twelve weeks!" The timeline isn't my goal; a powerful book is. And the clarity and confidence the author gets in their message during those two years is worth its weight in gold, because they're able to help others even more powerfully while standing taller in their own self-worth and convictions.

I encourage you to strongly consider writing with Compelling Compassion, because the end result will grow you into a better writer with a more powerful book. It will also help you evolve into a better coach/guide/listener. It's part of why *your* growth helps the world as a whole. When you grow, that energetic expansion touches more people. That's something that's not always quantitatively measured when it comes to sales numbers and income, but it's truly the most impactful result of you sharing your story and message with others.

THE MINDF*CKERY NOW LIKELY TO ENSUE

(AND HOW TO GET PAST IT)

You now have an understanding of the most important components to consider before writing the first draft of a powerful book. Just as I'm not bold enough to declare that I can write a book about *exactly how* to write a book, I'm also not bold enough to declare that my approach is the only one or the best one for everyone. However, it's certainly worked enough times that I'm confident in declaring that it's a viable option and one that's likely to get you where you want to go.

But (and it's a big but), as I've learned, the process sometimes needs a bit of...support. Because there are some nagging thoughts that will continue to penetrate your mind as you go through it, even beyond the eight I presented at the beginning of this book, which reflect the most common concerns people have before committing to write the book. Once you commit, other thoughts will arise. And those are the ones that often result in the manuscript being set aside for weeks, months, or years.

This is an aspect of book writing that I haven't seen covered in many books (or programs) that discuss the book-writing process. But it's the piece of book writing I love the most. Because it speaks to the aspects of *yourself* that you'll uncover while writing, while going through and growing through the challenges that come up. I will title each of the chapters in this section based on the way I've heard the "hiccup" commonly expressed. You may recognize some of these hiccups already, or they may become frighteningly familiar at some point in the near-distant future.

Let this section remind you that you are not alone. Not even close. Also, there is a solution for each of these challenges. You aren't unique (in having these concerns, anyway), and I know you can get past these glitches. If this book doesn't provide quite enough support, I encourage you to consider one of my programs or another book writing coach's programs from which you can get much more per-sonalized coaching through the muck. Doing so will impact not only your ability to get your book written but also your ability to work your way through other roadblocks and chal-lenges in your life.

CHAPTER 11

"BUT I DON'T KNOW WHERE TO START."

I know what you're thinking: "This all sounds great, Elizabeth. I totally get what you're saying about core message and knowing my reader and I've watched the workshop on creating my outline. You're bloody brilliant, and I'm ready to write now. *But how?*"

Sitting down with the idea that you're going to put all of your thoughts, experiences, insights, lessons learned, and recommended desserts to consume after I-made-it-through-this-shit moments onto paper can feel incredibly overwhelming. This is true even after you've created the outline that will serve as a blueprint through the process.

The blank page and the blinking cursor that sits at its top are daunting. And it's important that you know that that's true for writers both deeply experienced and not. We've been conditioned to see a blank page as a wide-open canvas onto which we have free reign to post all of our hopes and dreams. A blank vision board? Enthralling! A blank slate after a painful argument? Hallelujah! But a blank page onto which we're expected to write words in the best way to convey a specific thought or feeling? That results in "Anyone want ice cream?" Some people dream of showing up for a test for which they haven't studied. Some dream of arriving in a foreign country without a passport or any luggage. Some dream of sitting at a keyboard, staring at a blinking cursor. They're all equally drenched in sweat upon waking.

That was true for me even as I started this book. And it was true for the five books that I wrote and published before this one. (And for all of them, I had an outline to work off of.) I've talked to dozens of authors who have each published multiple books, and they confirmed that they also go through the same paralyzing cycle each and every time. Every single one of us ultimately has to muster what's necessary to sit down and just do it. There's no getting around the fact that, as I've said, the doing must be done. At some point, the how of writing a book stops being *in*structive and starts being *con*structive.

I recently interviewed Jessica Fein, whose memoir will be released in 2024. It would be an understatement to suggest that her subject matter wasn't easy or fun to write about at all times, and when I asked how she got the first draft out, she floored me with her straightforward response: quickly and poorly. It's truly the best way. I now have "Quickly & Poorly" written on a Post-it Note affixed to my laptop. So do several of my clients. Once you have something written—quickly and poorly—you can add to it, delete from it, and otherwise sharpen it. But as long as it's still sitting in your head, you've got nothing to work with.

It's truly not terribly different when it comes to anything else new and "nervousing." (I'm certain that I made up that word. Urban Dictionary recognizes it; fingers crossed that Merriam-Webster soon follows suit.) I'm a big DIYer around the house, and I remember the first time I used a nail gun. I was so nervous that I watched at least 87 YouTube videos showing me how to connect the air compressor, at what angle to hold the nail gun, which nails to use, how much pressure to apply, and what it was going to feel like when I pulled the trigger. At some point, I had to just pick up the damn tool and give it a go. My first few nails went in sideways. I didn't know to properly position the hole the air shoots out of (it was pointing right at my eye). And I'm lucky that a poorly aimed nail wasn't intercepted by the shin of an innocent bystander. But now, using that nail gun is second nature to me, *and* I'm always learning new ways to use it more efficiently.

When it comes to writing your book, at some point you have to stop reading books (oh the irony), watching videos, and listening to podcasts about how to write a book. You have to sit yourself down, stare that blinking cursor straight in the eyes, and say, "Let's do this thing."

Please don't assume that your approach to the doing of it has to be like anyone else's. Each of us has to figure out our own unique process. Some people write in a more rigid, journalistic way. Some write in a stream of consciousness manner and clean it up afterward. Some of my authors go for walks in order to get their content flowing, because do-ing so jogs their thought process. They take a voice recorder with them and record what they're thinking, then come home, transcribe it, clean it up, and go from there. The ed-iting of those transcribed sessions can actually be some-what fun, and it's far easier than getting the actual content out some of the time. Funny enough, if I try to voice record my thoughts while on a walk, I'm completely silent. It's like I'm standing on a stage in front of Shemar Moore, Ryan Reynolds, and Ryan Eggold, having been asked what my fa-vorite date night would look like. I've got nothing but...nothing. While dictation doesn't work as well for me, it's a successful strategy for many people.

I sometimes encourage my authors to record them-selves while speaking as though they're standing on a stage talking to a large audience (one that doesn't contain any of their celebrity crushes), or I prompt them with specific questions while in casual conversation and have them free-style answer. This works well because sometimes the mere thought of "Ohmigod, how am I supposed to address this? What's the answer that people want to hear?" can keep you from opening your mouth at all! You don't want to publish a book that's a mere transcription, obviously, but the first most daunting part of writing a book is unconditionally get-ting the content out of your head and onto the page. There are other daunting parts, but that's the first one, and once we get past it, we can move on to the next.

Figure out what works for you. If it doesn't work for you to get up at 4:00am and write, don't do that. If it doesn't work for you to write every single day, don't do that. But if you're going more than five to seven days without writing at all (without a major life event unfolding) and you're trying to convince yourself that writing once a month is "just my process," I'd challenge you on that.

There's a fine line between "It doesn't work for me to write every single day" and "I have to wait until inspiration strikes." If you're relying on the latter, you're putting control outside of yourself by saying, "When inspiration strikes, I will write." Know what's going to happen? Inspiration's never going to strike. Or it's going to strike once a year. Placing ownership or blame outside yourself rarely, if ever, works.

For this book, I committed to writing 2,000 words a day, five days per week, via whatever means necessary to get those 2,000 words out—and that was while managing five kids and working with clients and dealing with a dog who barks at the sound of a leaf silently falling from a tree three blocks away. This is to say that if I can find a way to make it work, I'm confident that you too can find a way to make it work. I type fast, so some days, I sit down and type. Some days, I do actually record content while driving to the store and then transcribe it later. There is something about driving that allows me to think less and talk more, which I should probably look into. It likely isn't terribly safe, but it works now and then.

There were weeks toward the end of writing this book that I did *not* write five days a week for a variety of reasons. I ended up sequestering myself in a hotel room in Sedona,

Arizona, for two days to get the last 15,000 words written before beginning my first round of edits. I knew I was *that* close and needed to just block out time (and the barking dog).

Despite what some suggest, writing a book isn't as simple as taking a weekend, doing a brain dump of any number of words, and then releasing the result of that into the world (and expecting it to be well received). Go big or go home. As a popular meme infamously states, "People who say 'go big or go home' greatly underestimate my desire to go home. Like, it's all I want to do." But when it comes to writing a book, the biggest step you can take is to commit to going big. If you don't, you likely won't see the result you hope for (or anything near it) on the backend.

When concerns pop up, remind yourself, "Elizabeth told me this was going to happen," and ask yourself what you need in order to work through those things, whether it's talking with a friend, reading another great book, going to see your therapist, hiring a coach, or joining a writing group.

Whatever you do, *don't shelve the book* and think, "When this issue passes, I'll get back to it." In all likelihood, whatever it is that you need to work through and the way that you'll work through it truly *needs* to go in the book. I won't necessarily suggest that that's why it's popping up, but it's absolutely a benefit of it happening. Be brave enough to go into it with an open heart and an open mind, and work through it so that you can then impact somebody else with the way you uniquely handled whatever it is you were challenged to handle.

Here is a reminder I encourage you to post on your wall:

Book writing is a process.
It will require work.
The work won't always be fun.
It will take time.
Fears will pop up.
I am ready to address them.
I am *able* to address them.
My story matters.
My message matters.
My insights will be someone else's favorite resource.

CHAPTER 12

"BUT SOMETHING CAME UP."

One of the first things I inform my authors is, "Just so you know, at some point during this process, something significant is going to happen, and you're going to want to quit working on the book." I don't mean necessarily that a meteor is going to crash through your roof. I just mean that something big enough to make you question what you're doing—and the rationale for doing it now—is going to occur. It could be that you get a promotion. Or decide to sell your home. Or your child suddenly needs a bit more support day-to-day. As a result, the gorgeous schedule you set forth for yourself when it comes to writing the book will, in some way, be interrupted or feel like it needs to be put on hold altogether.

When something like that occurs, it's entirely possible that you will decide that you have to stop writing the book immediately in order to tend to this "other thing," which, in some cases, is true. If someone in your family gets really sick or you break both arms, you may legitimately need to take a break for a moment. *But*, that doesn't mean that you have to take a break from living with your book in mind. Even when those things are going on and being tended to, I encourage my clients to keep journals or notes or whatever they can to remember what pops up for them during the "whatever" they're going through. As crazy as it may sound, the universe will absolutely put opportunities in front of you that can strengthen your resolve when it comes to the principles and philosophies you're putting into the world to positively impact others.

For example, if you're telling everybody to walk a certain walk when it comes to their money mindset, I wouldn't be surprised if your bank account balance lands close to zero at some point during the writing of the book, or you fear that it's going to for some reason (a big client threatens to cancel, big layoffs happen at your job, or the market completely plummets while all of your money is invested in Peloton). Or perhaps the absolutely impossible will happen, and something unprecedented will occur—say, a global pandemic.

The point is that one way or another, something will happen to either concretely encourage you to walk your walk, and/or you will question your ability to write a book without feeling like a fraud because you're actually struggling through the exact thing that you're trying to guide your readers through. I find it incredibly ironic that the one thing that most often keeps people from starting their book is incredibly similar to the thing their book is intended to get their readers through. It makes total sense—if you can't get yourself through the thing that you're encouraging everyone else to get through, you're out of alignment, and nothing flows from a non-aligned state. *You* have to figure that thing out—whatever it is—before you can guide others through a process of figuring it out for themselves.

Now, to be clear, stating that you've figured something out to the point that you can guide others through it isn't stating that you're perfect and can manage anything and everything until the end of time. It doesn't mean that, a year later, you can't have developed a slightly modified approach. What's critical is that what you believe to be true and the way that you behave based on that belief is accurate *at the time you're writing the book*. We all grow; we all evolve. I can go back and look at lessons or rules that I had for myself when I wrote *You Cannot Be Serious* twelve years ago that I don't necessarily subscribe to in the same way anymore, but that doesn't mean that they weren't true for me at the time, nor does it mean that I wouldn't encourage someone to adopt one of the principles today if it were an approach that worked for them.

Another reaction to something unexpected happening while writing a book is that people think, "I can't write the book until I figure *all* this stuff out." When they say that, what they're really saying is, "I can't write the book until I figure all of *life* out," and that doesn't happen until…well…you're dead. I don't know if it even happens then. There is a distinct difference between writing a book when you're in the eye of the storm and writing a book when you're on the other side of the storm, when you've gone through something and can unequivocally say, "These are the approaches that worked, and these are the approaches that absolutely did not work." In fact, you can write the book while you're *in* the fire as long as you don't leave readers hanging by not getting through the fire before releasing the book. The point of writing a book while you're in the fire is to effectively capture your fears, your questions, and your overall state of mind. But don't release that book until you can tell people, "This is how I felt *and* this is how I got through it."

CHAPTER 13

"BUT WHAT IF PEOPLE DON'T LIKE IT?"

L et me cut to the chase: some people won't like your book. To boil it all the way down to the bare, simple truth of an unfortunate but inarguable fact, you don't like positively everything you read, do you? None of us do! Therefore, the notion that everyone will like your book is a setup, and the idea that everyone *has* to like your book in order for it to be deemed valuable is absurd. There will be people who you really respect who won't love your book, and there will be people you don't even know who will flat-out *love* your book!

If you're in any way unsure about whether this notion is at all accurate, survey five or ten of your closest friends, asking each of them what they think about Crocs footwear or Starbucks coffee or the Spongelle bath sponge (which, for the record, is absolutely fantastic; the sugar dahlia scent is pure magic after a day of writing). In all likelihood, not everyone will respond in exactly the same way. Perhaps eight out of ten will like something, or seven out of ten will abhor something, but it's unlikely that all ten of them will absolutely love anything, and that fact won't make you respect or like them any less as a person, right? I have been known to say that decaf coffee is for losers, and anyone who doesn't like cupcakes is a psychopath. But alas, I now drink decaf coffee, and I have a fantastic friend who doesn't like cake in any form. So there you have it. If you say your book is for everyone, it's for no one, plain and simple. And if you fear your book is for no one, you're wrong, plain and simple.

Somebody might think your writing style is fantastic, but the topic of your book simply doesn't interest them. Somebody might be very interested in the topic of your book, but your perspective or solution doesn't interest them. Perhaps you're not funny enough, or you're too funny, or you provide too many statistics, or your book is too long (or too short), or you use too many big words and it makes them have to refer to their dictionary too often, or you swear too much, or you never swear and that makes you suspect in someone's eyes (read: mine). There are all kinds of reasons why someone might not like your book, but your focus absolutely cannot be on who *won't* like it; it must be on who *will* like it. Once you put your unwavering focus there, the rest will fall into place.

I have an extremely good friend who is a prolific author. I absolutely love her books as well as her writing style. So it made sense that I told her about a book I had read and fallen completely in love with. I highly recommended that she purchase it. She called me a few days later and said, "Elizabeth, I just cannot get into this." I couldn't believe it. I was completely shocked and said, incredulously, "What do you *mean* you can't get into it? This is the greatest book I've read in months!" But in her mind, it just wasn't that great. Yet that doesn't mean that the writing isn't good. It doesn't mean that the characters aren't well thought out. It doesn't mean that the structure isn't fantastic. It just wasn't her type of book. And that was the day I truly learned the lesson that just because someone—even someone who is a prolific writer or a very funny person or great with money or an incredible health coach—doesn't like your book does not mean that your book sucks. It just means that your book wasn't for them, and that's fine. You can't afford to spend any time focusing on the people for whom your book is not being written.

Accepting the fact that not everyone will like your book is incredibly freeing. Many of those with whom I work and to whom I speak are people-pleasers, and in full transparency, I'm very much a recovering member of that club myself. I've made great strides, but it still creeps up from time to time. I want everyone to like me, my writing, my hand-knit scarf, my hair, and my nail polish choice. For those who share that tendency, the desire for everyone to like our book—and the heart-wrenching discomfort we feel when one person doesn't—can be debilitating.

Most of us want people to like us. It's human nature. And once we can admit both that *and* the fact that not everybody is going to, and not everyone is going to like our book, we can begin to move through this debacle more gracefully.

Think about some of the most popular celebrities. They're either loved or not, for one reason or another. Some people worship the ground Cardi B walks on, while others wonder why on earth anyone is paying attention to her. Neither reaction or response has anything to do with Cardi B. They have to do with the person who has the opinion. Cardi B therefore shouldn't change a darn thing, because if she does, she's going to be constantly changing, and the goalpost is always going to be moving as she tries to make who she is work for everyone else, which is an actual impossibility.

Keep being who you are, keep putting your work out there, and keep striving to get it in front of the people for whom it will make a difference. You'll be a million times happier than you would be with the opposite approach.

CHAPTER 14

"BUT I'M WAITING TO FIGURE OUT THE TITLE."

I love a great book title more than I love just about any-thing in this world. I will buy a book simply because it has, in my opinion, an incredible title (or an incredible cover). When this happens, I don't even read the back cover. I don't research the author. I don't care if the book is 655 pages long. I must have it. So it stands to reason that I get a bit obsessive over my own book titles (and covers). But I have to rein myself in sooner than later, and you might have to do the same.

If it feels like writing an entire book is hard, let me fore-warn you that coming up with a title can feel earth-shatter-ingly difficult. There are a few instances when an author knows before he or she starts writing precisely what the ti-tle will be and never strays from it. But more often than not, people start writing books without any idea of a title. Or perhaps they have a tentative title idea, but a tenth of the way through think, "I don't like that title anymore," or see the exact title on another book, or tell someone the title and the person (who may very well be a stranger at the post office) doesn't light up, so they think, "Well, that title clearly sucks. Back to the drawing board."

I want to point out right here, right now, that telling people the title of your book is very much like telling people what you're going to name your child before the child is born. For some reason, if that child has yet to exit its mother's womb, people think they can interject their opinion with a level of passion that suggests that said opinion is of paramount importance when it comes to the child's future well-being.

"Do you have a name yet?" someone asks with a curious smile.

"We do!" you respond. "Her name is Catapult Grace. We're going to call her Cat."

In this moment, the person's only job is to muster every bit of delight she can before saying, "Wow! Wonderful! How unique!" Not, "Catapult? Really? *Are you sure?*" Meanwhile, you've had the entire nursery decked out with Catapult pillows and custom wall art from Etsy, and you have to run to the car to have a breakdown because what the hell is wrong with the name Catapult, and also, hormones. Meanwhile, the person who criticized the name Catapult typically just had a baby she named Tree, and the person criticizing your book title just released her first novel, titled *Alice in Thunderland*.

Just as we, as humans, want to be liked, we also want to be valued, and one of the ways we feel valuable is by "helping" if not outright "saving" someone by letting them know (completely unsolicited) that their book title (or baby name) is a really bad choice. It's as though we anticipate the person we've "saved" calling us up eight years later and saying, "God, thank you so very much for bringing my attention to how poor of a decision I was going to make. What would I do without you?" (To which the savior would respond, sheepishly of course, "Oh, it's nothing.")

As with the name you're considering giving your child, if you are not 100 percent confident in your title, do not tell more than two (three, max) souls what you're considering. Trust me on this. Having a thought partner for your book title is a great idea; surveying your entire Facebook friend group is not. Considering your title is important; obsessing over it is not. I can't tell you the number of times I've sat by (less than patiently) as writers defer the publication of their book, sometimes for months, because they simply "don't feel that the title is right." Or they survey 4,300 Facebook "friends" (4,280 of whom would not consider purchasing their book in the first place) and report, "They're split dead even between option A and option B—yet I prefer option C. Now what?"

I see many authors post a series of covers or title ideas on social media, asking friends and followers to vote on their favorite. This is a great strategy for one thing and a horrible one for another. When it comes to simply driving engagement and teasing that your book is coming soon, this approach is great. However, in terms of getting an actual scientific answer, it's horrible if the people voting aren't your target audience. If John likes the blue cover, but he won't be buying it, and Jen likes the red cover (and she will be buying it the minute it's released), you can't really say you have a tie. The fact that Jen will be buying the book gives her opinion far more weight. In the end, even among those who will become loyal readers, cover design opinions are just that: opinions. Same goes for the title and subtitle.

Again, people like to be heard. They like to contribute. They like to feel like they're part of a solution. And that's exactly what you're getting when you share four possible titles (or covers) with an audience and ask which most resonates. Now, if you're sharing them in a Facebook group that contains your ideal audience (with the permission of the group leader, of course), that may net you a far more constructive result. But a survey of random people does more harm than good.

At one point after releasing *Enough*, I put such a poll on Facebook. I was curious as to whether a different subtitle would be more appealing. I received several hundred votes, and while they were all over the map, the winning subtitle was the one I was already using. I can't say for sure whether things would have gone differently had the winner been another subtitle, prompting me to change it, because that didn't happen. But one fact that can be counted on until the end of time is: opinions are everywhere. Therefore, for the most part, you need to get comfortable with a title, subtitle, and cover that *you* love, then work outward from there. In fact, when I put the "new subtitle" poll on Facebook, one person responded, "Your book would sell far better if your cover had shades of blue on it." This was confusing, as I hadn't asked about my cover design at all. But were I more able to be swayed and less in love with my cover, I could have easily thought, "Oh! The secret is a completely redesigned cover!" when, in all actuality, it almost never is.

In many cases, the title of a book doesn't come forth until the book is being written, or even edited. A client of mine, Amy Westbrook, released her first book in 2020. When the book came my way, the working title was *Walking in High-Healed Shoes*, which was a great play on words but felt sterile, especially given how humorous, story-filled, and moving her book is. At one point in a later chapter, she had written, "I souled out" and we thought, "What a great title: *Souled Out!*" Indeed, that became the title.

The title is not the horse; it's the cart. You don't need a title to start writing. And you don't need to fret over the title for more than twenty-three days before you finally pick one and publish. If you take much longer than that, the title has simply become the latest way to procrastinate doing something you're afraid to do, which is put your book into the world and be confronted with the first person who's bold enough to say they don't like it.

CHAPTER 15

"BUT WHAT IF I DON'T SELL AS MANY BOOKS AS SO-AND-SO DID?"

I deas abound when it comes to how to determine when something or someone is successful. Maybe it's owning a home. Maybe it's having a million dollars in our bank account. Maybe it's hitting a $10,000 month. Maybe it's having a steady stream of clients. Maybe it's finally making a confident decision between Coke and Pepsi. (Maybe it's finally no longer caring how other people think it's defined and instead deciding what success looks like to *you*. Just a thought.)

When it comes to your book, you will also create a barometer by which to measure whether it's successful. This can be a tricky metric for someone who's never before written a book, which is why I suggest starting with something basic like "sell 100 books." Or sell one book to someone who doesn't know you and doesn't know anyone who knows you (i.e., a complete stranger), which is exactly what my goal was for my first book.

More often than not, I hear, "My goal is to sell 10,000 books," which, for the record, is completely doable. But 10,000 is also a pretty big number, and one does not reach that number without some significant effort, especially if he or she doesn't have a sizable platform of target readers to market to from Day 1. So start with something that feels reasonable *and* can be built upon. If your goal is to sell ten books, and you sell ten books on Day 1, you then raise the goal to fifty books. Then 200 books. Then 1,000 books. And so on.

The reason people so often have outrageous goals in terms of book sales is that they've seen a Facebook post that says something along the lines of "I sold 60,000 copies of my book in one week with no email list, no publicist, and no paid ads, and you can too (when you purchase my super simple system)."

Here's the issue with this: The person who's purporting that he sold 60,000 books often either did not sell anywhere near 60,000 books, or he gave away 60,000 books via Facebook ads (which cost him $10,000), or his best friend has a targeted email list of 1.2 million, and he "sold" a free copy—just pay the $4.95 shipping charge—to 60,000 of those people. This now-supposedly-rich-and-famous-but-actually-real-unclear-as-to-where-the-next-sale-will-come-from author is not necessarily straight-up lying, but the assumption that he sold 60,000 copies at full price (or anywhere near it) is false. I know authors who sell 1,000 books at $18.95 and therefore earn a higher net profit than those who "sell" 10,000 copies for an email address. It's frustrating that full transparency isn't sexier than it is.

I honestly don't spend a lot of time taking issue with any of this except for the fact that the misleading tactics in this and many other industries cause people such unnecessary angst. When someone says they've sold 100,000 books, but their book only has three reviews on Amazon, it's indeed possible that they sold 100,000 books through an event, trade show, affiliate partnership, or the like. The Amazon rating or number of reviews isn't necessarily indicative of a book's popularity or reach. However, if that individual has a heavy speaking tour schedule and you don't even have an email list, the likelihood that you're going to follow in his footsteps right out of the gate is slim.

Remember that people have different intentions when it comes to writing a book. For some, a book is part of their business model to further establish their credibility and attract new clients. For a long time, the saying "A book is the new business card" was all the rage. It rubbed me the wrong way then, and it most certainly still does today (even more so, in fact). A decade or so ago, that concept may have held slightly more weight because self-publishing wasn't nearly as accessible as it is today. But now, people whip out a 12,000-word book in a weekend, don't edit it, do a quick upload to Amazon, and are surprised when it not only doesn't sell but also performs ("as a business card") about as well as one printed onto cheap printer paper from your home office's ten-year-old printer (the one with extremely tired color print cartridges). In 99.967 percent of cases, 12,000 hastily written words creates a pamphlet that deludes itself into thinking it's a book but clearly isn't a book. I said what I said.

One aspect of the saying "The book is the new business card" that I do agree with is that the magical opportunities that writing a powerful book can allow for are endless. From speaking engagements to online course creation to coaching (one-on-one or in groups) to podcasts (that you're a guest on and/or host yourself) to radio shows and TV segments to having articles accepted by major magazines and websites to raising societal awareness and generating perspective-shifting conversations, being the published author of a powerfully written book opens doors far more effectively even than hiring an expensive publicist. The key is, you have to be proud to send your book off when it's asked for and confident that you're putting your best foot forward—metaphorically speaking—in the process.

I remember a story a friend told me about an author who used his "published author" status to convince a convention chairperson to allow him to have a booth at their large annual event in Las Vegas. Throughout the event, this gentleman approached person after person, saying little more than, "Want a copy of my book?" He handed out his book liberally, ostensibly hoping that each of these individuals (many of whom were the heads of their respective regional divisions) would want to fly him in to speak to their employees.

My friend was shocked when he was handed the book. It was so short that it barely had a spine; he was able to read the entire thing over the course of his eighteen-minute Uber ride back to his hotel. It had clearly not been edited or even proofread, and the content hadn't been thought through or organized in the least. It was, essentially, a glorified pamphlet. Not only did my friend never consider hiring this gentleman to speak to his employees, but he put the "book" into a trashcan on his way into his hotel. (I shuddered when he said that and did so again typing it.) This was truly a missed opportunity. This gentleman had a perfect chance to share his insights and his approach in a thoughtful way with so many leaders. To build rapport and show that he respected their time by providing them with value. Instead, he focused solely on being able to say, "I'm an author, so I'm an expert." Needless to say, it didn't work.

On the flip side, when you put thought and intention into your book—the same amount of thought and intention you'd put into anything you were passionate about doing well—the doors that become available to open to you are truly mind-boggling at times. Through writing my first book, which brought to the surface an array of subtopics I could speak to, I was able to book TV segments any time I traveled to a new city. I was asked to be the (paid) keynote speaker for several conferences. I had no problem being booked on dozens of podcasts and radio shows whose listeners were my target readers. (It was 2004, and radio was still a popular medium.) I was asked to run a group for new moms of twins at my local hospital. I started a membership site for parents of newborn twins.

When writing memoir, the options are just as limitless. Opportunities to create societal awareness and change by speaking about your story are much more plentiful when you can show that you're the published author of a thought-provoking book. These days, saying you're published by one of the Big Five publishing houses (Penguin Random House, Hachette Book Group, Harper Collins, Simon and Schuster, and MacMillan) still gives you undeniable clout. But as long as you've written something that's of the same quality as a book published by a reputable house, and you can clearly communicate how you can benefit a group of listeners or viewers with great information (as opposed to showing up simply to promote your book), TV, radio, and podcasts segments will be all too happy to book you as a guest. After all, that's *their* goal: create thoughtful conversation that their listeners and viewers will enjoy, be entertained with, or be inspired by.

For some, their book isn't part of a business model at all; they simply can't NOT tell their story or share their message. There are people who will say that you're crazy not to have a pay-shipping-only funnel or similar plan to leverage your book to generate $18 million. There are also people who will say that sharing your insights and wisdom with others is priceless. None of these thoughts are wrong. Where we get caught up is when we get into a space where we forget that our own motivation and intention is, in and of itself, enough, which is why it's so important to get clear on what our motivation and intention are from the beginning.

Start where you are. Build from there. As my friend Jenn Hanson-dePaula, who is an incredible book marketing strategist (find her on social media at @mixtusmedia) taught me, "Start simple. Get fancy later." Create reasonable goals. Compete with yourself and yourself alone. Remember that *not* everyone is telling the complete truth when it comes to their numbers. And also, book sales alone typically isn't the way someone makes their impact or their money. Both impact and income come from engaging with readers and continuing to build your audience so you can go on to do other things, whether speaking, creating courses, coaching, consulting, or writing more books.

CHAPTER 16

"BUT LET ME REVIEW IT...JUST ONE MORE TIME."

I remember a time several decades ago when I bought the newest book by an author who was, at that time, incredibly popular. He'd released his first book to wild acclaim, and therefore a second book followed shortly thereafter. I couldn't wait to get my hands on it.

Page One had a typo, which was unfortunate, especially given that we were only on Page One. But then, Page Two had two typos. Page Three had six. And Page Four wasn't even formatted. This was pre-internet, and I remember sitting down and handwriting the publisher a letter, saying in no uncertain terms that it was abhorrent that they'd let this book go to print because it reflected so badly on the author. I couldn't even finish it and vowed I'd never buy anything written by said author again. To this day, whenever he releases a new work (he's now written a plethora of books), I won't buy it, even though I'm sure that error was never again made.

In all likelihood, they had an enormous print run done overseas, given the popularity of the first book, and what were they supposed to do? Throw them all out? (In my opinion, yes, and have a few words with the proofreader or the person who sent the wrong file to the printer.) Instead, they just went with it and crossed their fingers that no one would notice or...I don't even know. It's like in the movie "Elf" when it was discovered that the publishing house's new children's book was missing two middle pages, and Walter Hobbs said he wasn't going to trash an entire print run because they forgot two main pages of the story.

A book with that many errors should never get within a mile of the printer, but thankfully, that doesn't often happen. There will, however, likely be an issue or two here and there. Editors are human, as are proofreaders, and the fact is that the human brain sees what it thinks it's supposed to see on the page, not what is actually there. As an exaggerated example that would hopefully never make its way through a print run without being caught by a proofreader, consider how easily your brain deciphers the following sentence:

S1M1L4RLY, YOUR M1ND 15 R34D1NG 7H15 4U70M471C4LLY W17H0U7 3V3N 7H1NK1NG 4B0U7 17

As humans, we are proficient at reading garbled

nonsense. While no one in the scientific community is yet completely sure why this is, Marta Kutas, a cognitive neuro-scientist and the director of the Center for Research in Language at the University of California, San Diego, surmises that "Context is very, very, very important." Context is used to pre-activate the part of our brains that helps us to determine what's coming next. Therefore, we sometimes assume that what comes next is what *should* come next, even though our assumption may not be correct.

Occasionally, therefore, the wrong instance of they're, there, or their is used, or an apostrophe is missing, or a word is missing altogether even though the proofreader (and sometimes the first fifty-nine people who read the book) didn't catch it.

Just a few months ago, one of my authors called me completely panicked because her book, which had just been released after going through no fewer than 894 proof-reads, had a word misspelled—in the table of contents of all places. Instead of "wrapped," the word autocorrected (or something) to "ripped." The software didn't catch it because "ripped" is a word, and somehow, some way, none of those 894 proofreaders caught it either. We all saw what we expected to see. Thank goodness we could go back and make the adjustment, re-upload, start breathing again, and move on.

Guess what? Even if this happens, it's okay. For one thing, if you are self-publishing, you can go back, make the corrections (or have them made by your formatter) just as we did with the aforementioned incident, and reupload to

Amazon or IngramSpark or whatever other service you are using for print and distribution. Every book printed or downloaded from that point forward will reflect the change. Trust me, I have one error (and it's not even an error depending on who you ask) in *You Cannot Be Serious*, and that book was released before Amazon had a quality print-on-demand platform, so I still have a couple thousand books under my stairs containing this error. It's likely that no one on the planet will notice it, but I know it's there, and it haunts me more than the memory of the ventriloquist clown my grandmother gave my sister one year for her birthday—the one that used to sleep in my sister's closet. Now you're perhaps traumatized as well just thinking about that visual, and I apologize, but yet I don't, because I really don't want to be alone with it any longer. It's an image one simply can't let go.

Every book published by every major publishing house has the occasional error. Last night, I found an instance of "thought" that should have been "though" in a Colleen Hoover book. I don't think anyone's worried about her sales being affected or concerned that they can't change it in the initial print run of sixty-seven billion copies. I'm also likely the only person on the planet who noticed it. I have an uncanny ability to see this stuff. Unless, of course, the error's in my own book.

Thankfully, I've never seen anything quite as egregious as the previously mentioned book by the author whom I vowed never to read again, but you can bet that Penguin Random House, and Simon and Schuster, and Hachette, and even the beloved Chronicle Books, which happens to be my very favorite, has this happen. And it's not the end of the world. Unless you are a perfectionist. And in that case, I understand you completely.

The other issue that's coming into play when an author says, "I just need to review it one more time" is perhaps obvious: they're afraid to let the book out into the world. What if the third paragraph of chapter 4 needs a smidge more clarification? What if the dialogue quoted on page 67 should include an additional sentence? What if the aquamarine pool float mentioned in chapter 21 should be described as teal? Or Pantone 17-3938 (the 2022 color of the year)? What if chapter 21 isn't necessary at all?

You're not going to get to the point where you believe the book is one hundred percent perfect, because there's no such thing. What you need is to know that, yes, you could change a word here or there, and you could certainly expand on a paragraph (if not seventeen) or explain a concept differently. It's still hard for me to go back and read portions of my own books. Even though they're out there and people are enjoying them, I re-read something and think, "I could have said that better." But that's true of literally every single book in publication, and it's the plight of every creative person. Yet if the book never makes its way into the world, it won't matter that you could have said it slightly differently, because no one will be reading it! Trust what you've created. Trust the editor you've hired to help you polish it. And then, get it out there already!

CHAPTER 17

"BUT IS SELF-PUBLISHING CODE FOR 'NOT GOOD ENOUGH'?"

Oftentimes—in fact, most times—when I talk to authors in the initial stages of writing their books, they have one clear goal for the moment they declare the book 98.786 percent finished: find a publisher. In many cases, people prioritize how to find a publisher over how to write a book, a fact I find fascinating but also understand all too well, because let's be honest, your ego is going to attempt to talk you out of writing a book in any way possible. Sometimes the latest and greatest approach it employs is suggesting, "You really think you can get a publisher? It's not even remotely easy. So just scrap the whole thing."

One of the main reasons people initially think they want

a traditional publisher (or a publisher they deem to be "real," even if it isn't Penguin Random House), is that they have a sense that if a "real" publisher believes in their book, that means that the book is good. And if it's good, it will sell. Newsflash: neither is necessarily true. The publisher who invests in a book is taking as much of a risk as anyone. Sometimes that risk pays off, and sometimes it doesn't. They may initially believe in your book concept, and they may believe in you as the author. But that belief (as well as their long-term loyalty) is often dependent upon the ultimate sales numbers.

Even if you're committed to traditional publishing at the outset, you can always decide to go a different route later on. Still, many people are hesitant to self-publish (or work with a hybrid publisher)—that is, until they understand what's truly possible these days for self-published authors or authors who choose to work with a hybrid publishing house.

Self-publishing has gotten a bad rap over the years for two primary reasons. One, the ability for anyone and everyone to publish did for books what YouTube did for singers. Everyone thinks they're Justin Bieber or wants to make a quick dollar, so there's a lot of pretty bad quality stuff showing up. Thankfully, even online retailers have upped their standards to keep a good bit of the crap off the virtual shelves. The second reason self-publishing is often frowned upon (at least at first) is that, as mentioned earlier, one of authors' big fears is that people will think that if you're self-published, it means that your book isn't good enough to get a big-name publisher. This is so far from true at this point it's incredible.

Brené Brown started as a self-published author. So did Margaret Atwood. And Ken Blanchard. And Robert Bly. And Beatrix Potter. And Jane Austen. And e.e. cummings. And Charles Dickens. And Willa Cather. And W.E.B. DuBois. And Edgar Allen Poe. And Marcel Proust. And Julia Cameron. And Henry David Thoreau. And Mark Twain. And Ernest Hemingway. Ernest Freaking Hemingway decided to take matters into his own hands. Need I go on?

The number of authors who are deciding to bet on themselves, not waiting for a corporate conglomerate to sign off on the value they are providing, and proactively putting out an incredible product rises by the week. And while Edgar Allen Poe and Ernest Hemingway couldn't avail themselves of them back in the day, there are so many incredible service providers ready to help these authors. Many of them—from editors to cover designers—once worked in the traditional publishing space, so they know as much about what they're doing as anyone.

There are many benefits to self-publishing these days (or author-publishing, as its occasionally referred to), most notably the author's ability to have full control over book design (cover, title, subtitle, interior formatting), retain full rights, have a shorter time to market, enjoy the ability to execute marketing strategies that don't have to be signed off on and aren't dependent on third-party participation, have easy access to author copies, and appreciate an increased profit margin. There are, of course, also benefits to traditional publishing and hybrid/professional publishing.

For the purposes of quieting concerns around self-publishing being code for "not good enough," that notion is proving less and less valid by the day. It's a viable, profitable business model, as evidenced by the fact that many authors (including authors who have previously been traditionally published—and very successfully at that) are dipping their toes into the self-publishing waters.

I'll talk more about the differences between various publishing models in the publishing section, but for now, please note that whether you publish with a traditional publisher, a vanity publishing, a hybrid publisher, or you self-publish, one thing is unequivocally true:

YOU MUST BELIEVE IN YOUR BOOK AND ITS ABILITY TO IMPACT OTHERS MORE THAN ANYONE ELSE!

Even if you're published by a traditional publisher, if you don't believe strongly in your book (and therefore don't talk about it much), it likely won't sell well. As a result, you probably won't get another deal with that publisher. So many people don't recognize how many traditionally published authors aren't selling many books at all while underestimating the traction self- or hybrid-published authors are getting by being creative, persistent, and patient.

These days, one need only look as far as Colleen Hoover to see how big a self-published author's brand can become. Even having sold more books than James Patterson and John Grisham (combined), she still opts to self-publish here and there, and she sells the rights to her traditionally published books to a variety of publishers (as opposed to remaining loyal to one, as has historically been the route many authors go). Her rise began when her first (self-published) book, *Slammed*, hit the *New York Times* Bestseller List in 2012, without the help of a massive marketing campaign or reviews from mainstream book critics. Yes, this is an exception, not a rule, but also, she was forty-two and living in a single-wide trailer, making $9 per hour as a social worker when she wrote *Slammed*. Six of the top 10 NYT bestsellers in October 2022 were hers. Someone has to be the exception, and while I wouldn't put all my eggs in that basket, there's no reason to consider the possibility that the next one might just be you!

I see self-publishing as code for "I believe in this book like crazy. Why not put it out there on my own and retain full control over content, cover design, title, and profit margin? I've done my due diligence and hired a great editor, and I'm committed to championing it without restriction!" If the self-publishing model feels "less than" to you, I encourage you to give some thought to why you feel that way. Not wanting to solely undertake the tasks associated with self-publishing, preferring instead to have a partner who can help bring your book to life, is perfectly understandable. But avoiding self-publishing because of a perceived stigma is a mindset I invite you to reconsider. It's no different from deciding to self-fund (bootstrap) a new business instead of soliciting venture capital firms. They're simply two different approaches, each of which has both pros and cons *and* can be successful.

"BUT WHAT IF IT DOESN'T MAKE AN IMPACT?"

If you want to make an impact, make an impact.
If you want to make lots of money, make an impact.
—moi

The amount of money we make is quantifiable, but the amount of impact we make isn't. The amount of money your book makes can be tied to how many copies it sells and how many opportunities or clients you generate as a result of having published the book. The amount of *impact* your book makes often cannot be tied to those same metrics, at least not in an apples-to-apples way.

Whenever someone declares that they want to be a bestselling author, I immediately ask exactly what they mean by "bestselling author." Their answer inevitably falls into one of two camps: they want to make a ton of money, or they want to help a lot of people. It's never really about the "bestselling author" title—it's about what that title represents in an author's mind. In the same way that "I got signed by Simon & Schuster" represents "success" in some authors' minds, the term "bestselling" often represents money made or number of readers (or both).

If you sell a copy of your book for $13.95 to someone who ends up enrolling in a course you offer for $2,000, it's perfectly reasonable to consider the ROI on that one book sale to be approximately $2,000. If, on the other hand, you sell 1,000 copies of the eBook version when it's marked down to $1.99, netting you a payday of around $600 (and assuming that most of those purchasers were just being kind or making an impulse purchase they soon forgot about, resulting in them never opening the eBook), you can say, "I have 1,000 readers" or "My book has impacted 1,000 people," but do you really have that many readers? Has your book really impacted that number of people? Hopefully you can see how the vanity metrics of this game, like any other, quickly become an asinine way by which to measure your book's impact.

When I interviewed my client and friend Cory Goodrich for my podcast, she told me an amazing story that perfectly illustrates the impact we have as creatives that we don't know about until years later (if ever). Cory is an actor, and after doing a reading for a new show she's performing in, a young man approached her and said he'd come to the reading specifically because he heard she was doing it. He'd seen her perform as Mother fifteen years prior in "Ragtime" and after watching her sing, he thought, "I can do this. I want to have a career in theater." Of course, until he told her this, she had no idea that anyone was even paying attention, let alone moved to make an important life choice after seeing her perform. But here was this kid who made a life-defining decision that day. When you're a creative person, you simply never know how or when your work is going to inspire someone else. Your book will absolutely impact *far* more people than you'll ever be aware of.

Anytime someone clarifies that they want to be a bestselling author because their intention is to make millions of dollars and they believe that the "bestselling" status ensures that, we have to do some conversating. First of all, the majority of authors will not get rich from book sales alone. It does happen (cue Hal Elrod, James Clear, and David Goggins), but as stated previously, they're the exception, not the rule, and I wouldn't encourage anyone to bank (literally) on being the exception. People do indeed make substantial amounts of money off the backend of a book—through courses, speaking engagements, coaching, workshops, monetized podcasts, and subsequent books. But more often than not, a book is simply a tool. It's a component of an arsenal that supports an overarching strategy, not the be-all-end-all of the strategy.

Most of the people I speak with equate being a "bestselling" author with selling a lot of books to people who genuinely want to absorb them. As a result, those books make a strong impact on their readers' lives. That is why they aspire to that status—they want to make that kind of impact. That is an intention I can always get behind without hesitation. In a delightful turn of events, with that level of impact usually comes a positive financial impact on one's bank account. Therefore, going into the process with the intention of making an impact can net you two amazing benefits, impact *and* income, whereas going in with one singular focus (income) often leads to disappointment (as it does in nearly any industry or with any product or service).

The idea that you can simply whip out a sterile, disorganized book; claim bestselling status; and watch your career and bank account skyrocket is incorrect. Remember, you aren't selling a book; you're selling a *solution* to a problem. Therefore, you have to *have* a solution to propose in a new way, and you have to want to truly help *solve* someone's problem in order for your book to make a true and long-lasting impact. Nobody's "whipping out" true, long-lasting impact.

There is a critically important message I encourage you to absorb when it comes to how and when that deep, lasting impact is made: *it's not your job to fix anyone or to save anyone.* Oftentimes, people wonder, "What if I put my whole process into a book, and it doesn't work for someone? Does that mean I'm a fraud? Should I give them their money back and also send a pony for their trouble?" This is where we return to the importance of respecting and honoring the reader's timetable I spoke about in the Compelling Compassion section of chapter 10, because it's worth expanding upon here.

Where someone else is in their growth isn't any of your business. It's truly not. You might *think* it's your business because the growth they experience as a result of reading your book or working with you can prove the value of working with you, but putting yourself on the leading edge of someone else's growth is pretty risky. Alternately, if someone is determined to stay stuck for any number of reasons, you don't *want* to push them through that, nor are you responsible for their choice not to take a specific step forward at any particular point in time.

Some people would suggest that the best way to support someone is to outright force them to make change through shame or guilt or some other heinous form of emotional manipulation. But I don't move that way. I've rarely (if ever) seen it work, because, in the end, people make lasting change when *they* decide it's time, not when someone else shames them into it. We have to let people retain their sovereignty when it comes to when and how they make moves. It's truly the most loving way to support someone's long-term growth, even when we're positively verklempt over their unwillingness to move forward.

Sometimes, people aren't in the right place to receive your message when they first hear it. This is why I read some books over and over again, *The Alchemist* being my favorite example. Every time I read it, I glean something new, because I'm at a new state in my own growth. Same with *Frequency* by Penney Peirce or *Trust Your Vibes* by Sonia Choquette.

Consider the last time you heard something for the eighth time, but the eighth time was when it finally clicked. Perhaps it was the way someone explained a concept to you, or perhaps you were just finally ready to hear whatever insight was being shared. I have a friend who gets awfully frustrated with me because he'll explain something in a way that doesn't initially make sense, so I disregard it. But fast-forward two years, and I'm suddenly calling him and saying, "You'll never believe what I figured out today!" I hear crickets on the other line while I explain before he says, "I literally suggested that that was the issue two years ago." I either wasn't ready to hear it then, or it wasn't explained in a way that resonated. And that's part of the magic of sharing your unique insights using your own experiences, metaphors, and word choices. They're going to land with someone who's been dying to have that insight but wasn't able to "get" it when it was explained by anyone else at any other time. I'd be willing to bet that you've had your fair share of conversations with people where they said, "I've never heard it explained that way!" or "Ohmigod, I think I finally get it!" Trust your ability to uniquely impact someone else's life. Because you've been doing it all along.

Bad reviews also cause some authors to feel like their book isn't having the desired impact. I've always found it fascinating that authors will get ten glowing 5-star reviews, and then one jackass will go out and post a 1-star review about which the author will spend a full day being ticked off instead of focusing on the ten glowing ones. Full disclosure, I've been the author who spends a full day being ticked off.

I think it's fully normal for us, in our humanness, to wonder why someone doesn't like us or would go out of their way to get in our way. But this is just how some people are.

If someone says, "Your book didn't work for me," it's possible that it just wasn't for them. It's also possible—if not probable—that they are saying that about a lot of other books too. When someone writes a particularly scathing, borderline insanity-fueled review, it's sometimes fun to click on their profile to see the other reviews they've written. They're typically not much different, further validating that their thoughts had nothing to do with what you wrote and everything to do with the fact that, astrologically speaking, all their planets are in retrograde, and their moon is rising in hell. What's important is that you are in integrity, offering whatever solutions and insights you can while being willing to walk beside them as they navigate their own journey. Beyond that, their reaction is none of your concern.

Consider this: if the core principle presented in *The 5-Second Rule* doesn't work for someone, does that mean that Mel Robbins is a fraud and should quit on her mission immediately? She's reportedly the highest paid female speaker on the circuit, earning $75,000 for forty-five minutes on stage, so I'm gonna say no. Does *Who Moved My Cheese?* have scathing 1-star reviews? You betcha. Does that make Spencer Johnson a "bad" author or leader? Having written a book that's remained a bestseller since 2006, is noted as "one of the best business books ever" by the *Daily Telegraph*, and is closing in on 17,000 Amazon reviews (averaging 4.5 stars), I'll also say no.

A reader might implement everything you suggest, a few things, one thing, or nothing at all. Or they might implement none of it today and all of it eighteen months from now, because again, so much of it has to do with where the reader is on her journey when she gets her hands on your book. Your only responsibility is to come from your truth, perspective, and experience. The rest is out of your hands. Be unattached to how much of it a reader chooses to incorporate or resonate with and how well it works in their life at any point in time, and just keep on keeping on.

CHAPTER 19

"BUT ISN'T BESTSELLER STATUS IMPORTANT?"

F air warning: I'm going to get on a bit of a soapbox here, but it's going to be very much to your benefit. I fervently believe in the power of your book—even if it never hits a single bestseller list. And I have oodles of examples of books that have never hit an official bestseller list but have either sold incredibly well or helped leverage the author's knowledge and experience in such a way that a thriving business was built on the backend. Disclaimer in place, here we go.

The publishing space has gotten to a point where bestseller status is, for the most part, bullshit. There are a few exceptions, including the *New York Times* bestseller list (though even that's debatable at times given that it's largely an opinion piece, but I doubt we'll see anyone turning their nose up at it anytime soon), *USA Today*, *Wall Street Journal*, and major Amazon categories. Those are well-respected accolades. While that status can be bought (for $50,000 all the way up to multiple six figures), books that come by those titles honestly have inarguably "earned" them through consistently voluminous sales periods. If the accolade is bought through gaming the system, the book likely won't have consistently high sales periods after the week when the purchased campaign landed it on the respective bestseller list, but that's the strategy the author has chosen. Many people don't recognize how many books—even eBooks priced at $1.99—have to sell in order to hit one of these major lists. It's typically far more than a few hundred! In some cases, the leverage a book gets by hitting one of these major lists, even when through a strategic campaign, makes a lot of people aware of the book, which then allows its sales to grow organically from that point forward. It's an expensive risk that sometimes pays off and sometimes doesn't, which is inherently true of risks, period.

When it comes to being able to declare, "I'm a bestselling author," please note that there are "bestselling" authors who can't pay their rent, and there are authors you've never heard of living in bona fide castles. Still, being able to say, "I'm a bestselling author," regardless of where that accolade came from, remains incredibly desirable. What lights me up (in a not-so-ecstatic kind of way) is hearing someone say, "I'm a #1 Amazon bestselling author!" at which point I look up their book, which has two reviews and is number 1,547,978 in the Amazon store. But they aren't lying. Their book *is* sitting at #1 on Amazon...in Knitting and Other Yarn Arts (even though their book is about removing sugar from your diet). The truth is that they've never hit a major best-seller list, and the list they've hit is in an Amazon category most people don't even know exists. Believe me, there are more obscure Amazon categories than you can imagine!

These "black hat" strategies for manipulating the system in order to claim bestseller status have been around for years, and more and more people are getting wise to them. The phrase "I'm a bestselling author" is therefore not terribly well recognized anymore unless you're in the top 100 of the Kindle section or paperback/hardback section of Amazon, or you're in the top 10 in a major category (and by major, I mean Memoir, Fiction, Women in Business, or Finance. In other words, a large category where you have to sell a sizable number of books in a single day in order to have a shot at cracking the top 10 for even an hour). It is possible to do. *Enough* managed to remain at #3 for several hours in Women in Business, which I believe was the result of having a solid launch strategy and a pretty large launch team helping me spread the word (also, the stars properly aligned, no major news event usurped my planned launch, and Mercury wasn't in retrograde). But once the launch push died down, its #3 status quickly plummeted, and I had to (and still have to) consistently work to keep the book top-of-mind for people.

My good friend Drew Linsalata and I talk about this concept a great deal. Drew is the author of *The Anxious Truth: A Step-by-Step Guide to Understanding and Overcoming Panic, Anxiety, and Agoraphobia,* which has absolutely ended up on various Amazon bestseller lists from time to time but hasn't hit the *USA Today*, *Wall Street Journal*, or *New York Times* list. Regardless, he sells more and more copies by the month. He has an audience that grows by the day, thanks to his incredibly active Facebook group and podcast by the same name. He's in the trenches with his readers and followers every single day. He consistently nurtures and supports them with Compelling Compassion (he's one of the best I've seen at this). As a result, whether it's the paperback, the eBook, or the audiobook version, he continues to sell more and more copies. Further, he opted to price his paperback at $21.95, which is definitely the high end for books in that space. But it's so widely recommended that once people hear how incredible it is, they are more than happy to pay that price. I won't be surprised if his book ultimately hits one of the bigger lists organically, but he's never once suggested that if he hit one of them, he'd be selling more, and he rarely (in fact, I don't think I've ever seen him do it) mentions it when he does hit a bestseller list on Amazon. His focus is on serving and growing his audience.

At the end of the day, what authors choose to do with regard to declaring their "bestseller" status isn't my main concern. To each his own. My concern is the *real* challenge those declarations cause, which is thus: when authors declare, "I'm a bestselling author," everyone automatically assumes that they're selling thousands and thousands of books (and making thousands and thousands of dollars) when that's not necessarily the case. Further, they think they're doing something wrong because their book isn't having that same level of success. The fact of the matter is, you can simply say, "I'm a bestselling author" and not have to prove it. If, on the other hand, you say, "I'm a *New York Times* bestselling author," people are probably going to expect you to be able to prove that. The loosened parameters have allowed anyone and everyone to declare that they're something they aren't, at least not in the traditional sense. The best news is that there are plenty of authors making four and even five figures a month off book sales or related products and services who have never hit an official (reputable) bestseller list.

The moral of this story is: don't get hung up either believing that achieving bestseller status for seven seconds in an obscure category will make your career, or that never hitting it anywhere will break it. Neither is true.

CHAPTER 20

"BUT WHAT KIND OF EDITING WILL I NEED?"

I truly cannot tell you the number of times I've heard people say, "I'm a pretty good writer. I don't think I need an editor." Trust me, you need an editor. All (actual) bestselling authors have editors, and there's good reason. You are simply too close to your own work to see gaping holes in content, probable misinterpretations of what you said versus what you meant to say, and grammatical errors that can truly mess with your credibility if not caught.

While editing is a book topic in and of itself (the best resource I've found is *Intuitive Editing* by Tiffany Yates Martin, especially for memoir), I'll dive just deeply enough into the process to give you an overall sense of what you need and where to get it. There are three types of editing that I suggest authors get: developmental editing, copy (or line) editing, and proofreading.

In a developmental edit, the editor is focused on

revising or reshaping the manuscript when it comes to the overall structure, flow, and messaging. The editor will make sure that the book flows well in terms of the overall message you are trying to convey, and that your tone and voice are consistent and a good fit for your target audience. They'll ensure that you haven't given too little attention to one topic or too much to another. This is where they may recommend moving chapters around, combining chapters, moving pieces of content from one chapter to another, outright deleting content, or adding in new content to better support a concept or story.

In the copy (or line) edit, the editor is focused on the mechanics of your manuscript: punctuation, grammar, spelling, incorrect facts, glaring typos, and ways to reword a sentence whose meaning may be misconstrued. The focus is on making sure the book is as readable as it can be, line by line, once the overall content has been honed.

Proofreading is the final step, and I recommend that you use someone other than your editor for proofreading. Your editor will have reviewed the manuscript so many times by this point that his or her eyes will see things that aren't on the page (but should be) and gloss over things that shouldn't be there (the same word twice or the wrong instance of there, their, or they're) simply because the brain sees what it thinks it should (remember the sample sentence in chapter 16). It's perfectly fine to have a friend or family member (or four) do your proofreading for you. It's not something you have to hire out. Just remember to clarify exactly what you're looking for from them. This isn't an opportunity for a proofreader to say, "I disagree with the way something's said in chapter 4" or rework seven sentences in chapter 8. It's simply to say, "This word is spelled incorrectly" or "You're missing an apostrophe here."

The best way to find a great editor is by asking others who they recommend. Be sure that the people you're asking have written a book in the same genre you're writing in, as a fiction editor may not be the best fit for nonfiction (or they might; it depends on their area of focus), and an editor used to working on Ph.D. dissertations and science-based works may not be the best fit for a sarcastic, witty book on sex after sixty.

Other great resources for finding a top-notch editor include Reedsy and the Editorial Freelancers Association. You can check out their vetted editors and other resources via their respective websites.

CHAPTER 21

"BUT WHO DO I GET FEEDBACK FROM (AND WHEN)?"

A funny thing about writing a book is, even though we state that one of our biggest fears is that no one will read it, we rarely truly believe that it will be read by absolutely no one. On one hand, we have an irrational fear that no one will read it, while on the other we fantasize about thousands of readers posting beachside pics of them holding our book along with the hashtag #bestbookever. The moment of acceptance that someone (or many someones) actually *will* read it tends to freak people out, so as we stand on the shoreline preparing to tiptoe into the vast, turbulent ocean of readers, we wonder who's safest to share with first. In other words, we begin to consider who will encourage us to wade into deeper waters, not go running back toward the shore where someone's waiting to hand us a sippy cup filled with White Claw.

It will surely come as no surprise that once a writer gets more than halfway through the writing, the question "Who should I share this with…and when?" takes center stage. Obviously, at some point, you're going to share the book with others. Perhaps the first share will be with a group of beta readers, and perhaps it will be with your editor. In most cases, I am of the opinion that you should share your book with *very few people* before it's officially available for public consumption, and those you do share it with should be chosen with solid reasoning and a clear process for soliciting feedback.

The majority of the time, whether you realize it consciously or not, the underlying reason you will initially want to share your work with someone else is to hear, "This is amazing. You are amazing. It's going to sell millions!" I don't judge that motive for one second because I've been there, and I'm right back there again every time I write another book. Another reason people want to share their book is to get honest feedback, which also makes perfect sense. With those two intentions in mind, here are my suggestions when it comes to creating a share plan that results in upgrades to the book, not downgrades to your self-esteem.

If you choose to share your manuscript with beta (or pre-publication) readers, I suggest that you do so *after* you've worked with your editor. For one thing, your editor will clean up the vast majority of "This entire paragraph makes no sense" issues, which makes for an easier read for beta readers. When considering with whom you want to share your manuscript post-edit, please take a moment to consider why you're choosing each person to be part of the beta-reading team.

I tend to group beta readers into two categories. First, there are what I call pat-on-the-back readers. Second, there are target audience readers. The first group gives you the validation you might unknowingly be seeking, while the second helps with the upgrades you're open to receiving. Yes, some readers might fit into both categories.

For the most part, your friends (and possibly some of your family members) are your pat-on-the-back readers. We tend to expect them to be the kindest of our beta readers, and many times they are, but they can also be our greatest critics. Sometimes that criticism comes unexpectedly, which is another reason it's important to be clear with yourself about why you are choosing someone to be an early reader. It's also important to acknowledge up front that people's reasons for liking or not liking your book's content, structure, tone, or flow are not always about what they appear to be on the surface! (This is another reason to have your manuscript edited by a professional first; he or she will flesh out all issues related to structure, tone, and flow, so you won't be asking beta readers for feedback on that.)

If you're just getting started sharing your work and need some validation, by all means identify someone you believe will sing your praises. However, remember that that's their role, and refrain from declaring, three months later, "Aunt June said the book was incredible. Why has my editor torn it to shreds?" (And later, "Why am I not getting millions of sales?") Aunt June's role was to validate you as an author—no more, no less!

This brings me to the next category: early readers who can give (and from whom you can receive) constructive criticism. These readers are of paramount importance. The most valuable constructive criticism will come from people who are target readers of your book. Think about it this way: if your book is about removing sugar from your life, and you ask a friend whose social media profile picture is a super-sized Cinnabon to have a read-through, her feedback may be that the book didn't keep her terribly engaged. But it's not reasonable to expect her to be engaged by a book about something she has zero interest in!

Despite my suggestion to hold off on beta readers until you've gotten through a round or two of edits, when I spoke with the amazing Tyler Merritt about his process for writing *I Take My Coffee Black: Reflections on Tupac, Musical Theater, Faith, and Being Black in America* (which is so good it's borderline unfair), he explained that he sent each chapter—as he was writing it—to a group of beta readers he trusted. I nearly passed out upon hearing this, but clearly this approach worked for him, so I was curious to learn more about how he managed dissenting opinions about what people liked, didn't like, and were absolutely throttled by. Given that the first draft was approximately 138,000 words and more than 40,000 were removed, surely there were more than a few opinions that impacted which of those 40,000 words were removed. And surely, those opinions were not always the same.

Remember when I suggested having a clear process for soliciting feedback from early readers? I advise authors to explicitly tell their beta readers exactly what kind of feedback they're looking for by sending a list of specific questions to answer (likely no more than ten). This prevents them from going hog wild with their comments and sending a bunch of thoughts that only make you more confused. In Tyler's case, he asked each beta reader to tell him five things they *loved* about each chapter they read. When more than two people said the same thing, he knew that was a strong component that would stay in the book. The reason this approach works so well is that you could also ask, "What are three parts of the chapter you didn't feel were necessary?" and get five or ten completely different answers. At that point, it's up to you as the author to decide whether you want to keep those pieces in play. Remember, it's *your* book. If all ten of your beta readers (assuming you have ten) say, "I don't like the paragraph about how you like gummy worms because gummy worms are the worst thing ever," you have the right to say to yourself, "Well, gummy worms are a huge part of my story. They're staying."

The way I see it, this approach allows you to take a level of ownership that gives you increased confidence. So when Jimmy Fallon asks me why I brought up Jolly Ranchers in chapter 5 (when he interviews me on his show—it's my dream now that Ellen is off the air; let me have it), I get to say, "You know, I love that question, because one of my beta readers, who shall remain nameless, said I shouldn't admit to my love for yellow Jolly Ranchers. But I'm ready to own that aspect of myself. So I left it in." Taking that level of ownership over your own voice is more valuable than feeling safe that everyone will like it, which is, of course, impossible. Listen, all ten of your beta readers might say, "I love the story about how you got stuck in the mud" and you'll be feeling uber-confident about it—until review number seven comes in and says, "The story about you getting stuck in the mud was completely stupid, and it ruined the entire book for me." This is why it's imperative that you own every word, every story, every insight, and every perspective. Once you do, review number seven will only bother you a teeny bit (just keeping it real).

Because I believe I know your thought patterns pretty well, I'm confident that a question now swimming around your brain is: "What is the *exact* right number of beta readers?" The number of people you ask for feedback is truly not something to stress about. There is no magically perfect number, but I typically advise between three and eight. You could ask the "smartest" ten people you know (who also are target readers) for their input, and their input could differ significantly. Someone might think that chapter 5 is irrelevant. Someone will suggest a different introduction. Someone will suggest that you remove the introduction altogether. Someone will think you use too many em-dashes. Someone will think the book ends abruptly, while someone else will report that it's the best conclusion they've ever read.

Whether you have four or 400 beta readers, when

there's that much differing opinion, it's easy to go into a tailspin over whose suggestions are good, whose are bad, and why you ever thought you could do this to begin with. So stay on the side of fewer beta readers, have a clear process for getting the most helpful feedback, and trust yourself to make the best final call for *your* book.

Once your editor and beta readers have finished offering suggestions and you've incorporated those suggestions (or not), I advise that you get proofreading help from up to five people. These do not have to be target readers, but it's helpful if they are because having an interest in the material causes them to pay closer attention. Again, be clear on your expectations—you're looking for help with typos and missing words, not flow, content, or style. Everyone wants to be helpful, and everyone enjoys weighing in with their opinion. If you give people an inch, they'll take a mile in this area. They mean well, but without staying solid in where you are in the process, what you're looking for from proofreaders, and where their unsolicited feedback is coming from, your brain can easily work its way into a paralyzed tizzy.

No matter how great your book is, remember that there will be people who won't like it, or won't like a part of it. One of your proofreaders or friends may be one of those people. After *Enough* was published, someone close to me said, "It's a great book; I loved it. But if you ever do a second edition, could you remove the word 'motherfucker' from it?" No. No I could not. As it turned out, a sentence incorporating that word is one of the most-often highlighted portions of the eBook! But if I'd been more nervous about people's opinions, I might have taken it out.

Many times, authors I work with say (when we are on the cusp of publication), "I need to change something in chapter 3." When I ask why, they respond, "Because I was talking to somebody, and they said they didn't like a specific sentence. It was too snarky, or it didn't make sense, or...whatever." So they want to change it. My next question is always, "Do you want to change it because you *agree* with their feedback, or because you're *afraid* of their feedback?"

Feedback is great, both before and after the book comes out. Listen to the feedback, be open to it, and work *really* hard not to take any of it personally. And remember, people who provide feedback without having been asked for it are a breed in and of themselves, and I almost always advise putting an energetic bubble around yourself and thinking about something else entirely while they're talking. Then, politely say, "Thanks! I'll take that into consideration!" and walk the hell away.

On the other hand, if you ask someone, "What did you think of the book?" and they respond, "Oh my gosh, I totally loved it. Honestly, there was a place in chapter 3 where I was a little confused; there was a bit of a gap in the information," and you go back through that chapter and think, "I totally see what they're saying. I *did* leave a gap in the information," and you want to add to it a little bit, that makes perfect sense. And, by the way, this is a wonderful time to be self-published and have full control over your ability to go in and add a sentence or a paragraph here or there and re-upload the changes to your chosen distribution channels instead of having 3,000 copies in your garage that all have a slightly unclear paragraph in chapter 3 that you're now losing sleep over.

Still, make no mistake, it's just one person's opinion. If the feedback allows you to make the book better overall, super. But if you're making changes every five minutes based on the feedback of one person here and one person there, I encourage you to be more mindful about why you're so frantically changing things. If you have a good editor (and if you follow my advice, you will), you aren't going to have that many gaping holes, if any, in the manuscript. If someone says, "Well this joke wasn't funny" or "This story made me laugh too hard, and I almost drove off the road," a perfectly acceptable response is, "Well, *you're* not funny" or "Maybe you shouldn't be reading while driving." A perfectly acceptable response is *not*, "I have to change this part of the book or take this part of the book out because I might get sued by someone who was pulled over for weaving between lanes."

Another concern people have when they're getting ready to send out manuscripts for beta reading or proofreading is, "Do I need to watermark it or have people sign an NDA or formally copyright the manuscript first?" First of all, if you're sharing the manuscript with anyone you think might be even remotely capable of taking your work, turning it into a book, and putting their own name on it, perhaps don't ask them to proofread it. I have never felt the need to ask any of my proofreaders to sign an NDA or otherwise proactively protect my work. I've always chosen editors, beta readers, and proofreaders I completely trust.

When it comes to copyright, your work inherently has copyright. If you are spectacularly nervous, you can print out a full copy of your manuscript and mail it to yourself. When you receive it, DO NOT OPEN IT! Should you ever have to prove in court that you own the material, this post-marked, unopened envelope will serve as proof that, as of the date of the postmark, these were your words. Once your work is published, you can register it with the copy-right office if you'd like to. (In the interest of transparency, I'll again note that I'm not an attorney, let alone an intellec-tual property attorney, but this suggestion has been made by more than a few people who are.)

That's the low-down on your advance reader team. You have a professional editor, beta readers, and proofreaders. Once you get the final green light from your proofreading team, your book will be ready to make its public debut.

CHAPTER 22

"BUT HOW DO I GET REESE WITHERSPOON OR CHRIS PRATT TO ENDORSE IT?"

I f I've not yet mentioned it, I'm a big dreamer. True story: when Cory Goodrich and I released *Folksong: A Ballad of Death, Discovery, and DNA*, we dreamed of getting it in the hands of Reese Witherspoon. To the point where Cory's husband, David, Photoshopped an image of the cover into the hands of Reese, who was sitting on a park bench holding another book entirely. It was my screensaver for months. I haven't lost hope, but I change my screensaver as often as I rearrange my desk position in my office (which is often), and it was time. If you're someone who dreams of getting a testimonial from someone famous the world over, I support you! Also, let's talk about how to go about this.

People use the terms endorsement and testimonial interchangeably, but most of the time, in both cases what they're referring to is a blurb that validates that "this book is awesome, and you should buy it." The main difference between a testimonial and an endorsement is that a testimonial is given freely (not paid for), while an endorsement is paid for. Because they're paid for, endorsements often come with other components, like one or two tweets or other social media posts by the person who has supplied the endorsement. How far that goes when it comes to generating sales and awareness of you and your book remains to be seen on a case-by-case basis. (Sidenote: I've never advised anyone to pay for an endorsement of their book.)

"How do I get a blurb from a 'big name'?" is a common and understandable query. And whilst I do dream big, I'm also a practical realist when necessary. Keep the dreams, but when it comes time to go for testimonials, I encourage you to also be a practical realist. Make a blurb/testimonial wish list with three separate categories: dream, stretch, and likely.

Your dream list will include people like Oprah, Ellen Degeneres, Gary Vaynerchuk, Gwyneth Paltrow, Gabby Bernstein, and, if you're like me, Sandra Bullock, Amy Poehler, and Melissa McCarthy. Your stretch list might include people who are well-known in a specific space, but perhaps you have a connection to them, or you are willing to be curious about how inaccessible they really are. In this day and age, everyone is more accessible than ever, and while most big names get requests all the time from people to review their products, many of them also don't get as many as you might think (because everyone assumes they are inundated) and/or they are willing to help someone else who puts time and effort into making a genuine connection. Your likely list would include people who are likely to provide a testimonial, such as colleagues, friends of colleagues, professional acquaintances, and mentors.

While people get understandably sidelined thinking of what mega-influencer they might be able to get to blurb their book, the truth is that, sometimes, that mega-influencer isn't the right choice to begin with. For example, if you've been listening to Gary Vee for years and want him to blurb your book, but your book is about urban gardening, the number of people in Gary's orbit who are into urban gardening is likely far lower than, say, the number of people in the Gangster Gardener's orbit. (Never heard of the Gangster Gardener? His name is Ron Finley. Look him up. He's unbelievable.) You'll get far greater reach by having someone who's an influencer *in the space of your book topic* blurb your book than someone whose audience could, for the most part, not care less about the topic you're covering. If they were to agree to blurb it, you'd get super excited, expect massive reach and return, and then likely be pretty disappointed when very little came from it.

I ask my authors, "Who's a well-known person within your space?" and then recommend that they approach them for a testimonial. I never say, "Don't shoot for the moon," but I do recommend that you also approach someone who's perhaps a bit lesser known in your space than someone who is extremely well known to the vast majority of the world.

No one is known by everyone. I once mentioned Brené Brown to someone, and they asked, "Who's that?" I was floored but also excited, because that confirmed that even Brené Brown still has new people to reach! Same with Marie Forleo. And probably even James Patterson. Just last week, someone asked me if I'd heard of Colleen Hoover, because she hadn't until that morning. While I was surprised that she hadn't been sucked into the #CoHo phenomenon yet, I myself was only first sucked in a few weeks prior. Don't assume that just because you know who certain influencers are, everybody else does as well.

My client Janet Philbin wrote her book, *Show Up for Yourself: A Guide to Inner Growth and Awareness*, about inner child healing (both it and she are fantastic, if that's an area that interests you). A student of Dr. Shefali Tsabary, she asked Dr. Tsabary to write the foreword to her book. This is a name I suggested she put on her stretch list, because even though she had a personal connection to her, Dr. Tsabary is extremely well-known, and I therefore assumed she receives such requests frequently.

Not only did Dr. Tsabary agree to write the foreword, she also posted about it (unsolicited) on social media. Keep in mind, there's a benefit to the person providing a testimonial as well. As long as the book is "good" and they're truly endorsing something of value, it helps to continue getting their name out there too. Even though she has 687,000 Instagram followers, I had no idea who Dr. Tsabary was before Janet mentioned her to me. I immediately began following her and absolutely love her content. There's always a new reader (or mentor) to be found!

Another client of mine wrote a book and wanted someone who was well respected in the space to write the foreword, so he asked Annie Grace, bestselling author of *This Naked Mind* (whom I'd also never heard of before he mentioned her). She agreed. For both of these authors, those forewords held far greater weight in the community they were speaking to than a "bigger" overall—yet unrelated-to-the-niche—name would have.

Keep in mind that if you choose to self-publish, you can add testimonials later. Another of the many benefits of the self-publishing model is that if you get a killer testimonial a month after publication, you can simply re-upload your manuscript, and each book that prints from that point forward will contain the testimonial. If the testimonial is from a reputable enough source, you can even have your cover designer amend the cover to include it and re-upload that to your chosen distribution services. You can also amend your Amazon listing to include new testimonials as they come in, and you can certainly feature new testimonials on social media and in emails to your subscribers. So, while it's ideal to get these testimonials before pub day, you aren't completely sunk if you don't.

As far as when to send out requests for testimonials, I suggest asking potential endorsers two to three months before you plan to publish in order to give people appropriate time. And be sure to give them a deadline. Without a deadline (and a reminder or two), they will likely forget. Don't take it personally; you'd probably forget too! Most people will want to read at least a portion of the book before providing a blurb, so I suggest sending them an electronic PDF copy of the book. No need to watermark it or copyright it. If you distrust them that much, don't ask them to endorse it in the first place! They will likely simply skim the manuscript to get the general gist of what you're saying in order to ensure they're comfortable endorsing it because their credibility is on the line too.

In some cases, you can pay media outlets like Kirkus Reviews to review your book. But it's not inexpensive, so you have to determine whether or not the value you're getting in return makes the investment worthwhile. Getting reviews from outfits like "Publishers Weekly" or any major magazine is difficult for an indie author without a publicist or a connection who has a relationship with an editor at those publications.

Truly, no one testimonial or media hit will make or break your book. Many people are surprised to learn that the average appearance on "The Today Show," which has millions of viewers, nets only about 350 sales. A few hundred books sold is nothing to sneeze at, nor is the credibility garnered from having been a guest on such a show. But when you compare the average book sales numbers to the millions of people who are actually watching the segment, you recognize how small of a percentage it actually is and can go into the opportunity, should it present itself, with your expectations properly set.

CHAPTER 23

"BUT WHAT ABOUT BOOKSTORES?"

It's possible that you won't meet a person who loves bookstores more than I do—unless it's my friend Heather. Especially indie bookstores—my devotion to them runs deep. When it comes to big chain bookstores or the book sections of big box stores, however, I love them as a reader. As an author? Not so much.

To be clear, being carried in a bookstore is not the validator of whether you have a good book. There are amazing books gathering dust all over bookstores. Just look at the clearance racks! Nevertheless, "How do I get my book in bookstores?" is a question I'm asked by every single person I've ever spoken with who wants to write a book. Every. Single. One.

While I've not been traditionally published, I *have* had my books carried by both Borders (RIP) and Barnes & Noble.

The truth is, as an independent or self-published author, you do have the ability to get yourself into the same bookstores that traditional publishers can get their authors into. You simply need to know how to do it (and then decide if you actually want to once you understand the inner workings of it all).

Ready to dive in? You might want to grab a coffee, a brownie, or a stiff drink. This part of the industry can get a little confusing, but I'm here to help you make sense of it.

Bookstores (the big ones) insist on buying from a wholesaler. The main wholesaler in the U.S. is Ingram. Ingram offers bookstores two primary benefits that nearly every bookstore insists on: a 55 percent discount and a return policy (typically ninety days). For the record, KDP (Kindle Direct Publishing, which is Amazon's self-publishing arm) does not allow for wholesale returns. So even though KDP alleges that their Expanded Distribution program allows bookstores to order from them, they most often will not because KDP doesn't allow returns. They also don't offer the required 55 percent discount. Further, Amazon is every bookstore's (and almost every other store's) greatest competitor. So on principle alone, it's entirely possible that many bookstores wouldn't order wholesale from Amazon, even if they were to allow returns and offer the standard 55 percent discount.

The workaround for this for self-published authors is to upload their books to IngramSpark, which is a division of Lightning Source, a print-on-demand service that provides access to the largest global book distribution network of wholesalers, retailers, and booksellers, including Ingram (and other international wholesalers). In total, authors have access to 39,000+ retailers through this distribution network (though in truth, the likelihood of even a smidgen of a fraction of those picking up and stocking a book is quite low).

At the highest level, the way the process works in the traditional publishing world is as follows. A salesperson shares an upcoming release with the decision-maker at the bookstores. If that person agrees to take a chance on a new release, they order two copies, which are then typically placed spine-side-out on the shelf (in other words, *not* on the front table every author sees immediately upon entering their favorite bookstore and imagines their book sitting atop). Customers have to know your book is in the bookstore in order to purchase it. Yes, there are instances where someone just happens upon a book that's in the "stacks," but unless the book has gotten solid local press, it's not common.

Once the book is on the bookstore's shelf, it has eighty-nine days to sell. With the ninety-day return policy, any books that haven't sold after eighty-nine days will be returned to the distributor or destroyed (which is why most hybrid or vanity publishers that have a financial interest in sales don't pay author royalties until ninety days post-sale). In some cases, they may be put on the sale rack if the bookseller believes they can recoup some of their investment.

When I had books being sold by Borders, the pressure I

felt to know what bookstores were carrying my books so that I could let people know almost made me lose my mind. The books almost inevitably were returned to the distributor every eighty-nine days, and the shipping cost both ways was born by yours truly. In the end, *it cost me money* to have books in the big bookstores, and trying to understand the accounting ledger sent to me from my distributor was an absolute nightmare.

Obviously, if you're with a traditional publisher and they can get your book stocked in the bookstores, you go with it. If sales begin to dip, so will orders from the booksellers until you're primarily selling via Amazon or some other method. Early on, the majority of my books were sold in bulk to programs for expectant parents of twins and higher-order multiples. They weren't one-off sales in bookstores. And once Amazon came around, that's where 99.867 percent (not an exact number) of my sales have continued to be. Love 'em or hate 'em, sixty to eighty percent of consumers purchase their books from Amazon—sometimes even when they're *in* the bookstore! I hate to admit it, but I've found books that looked interesting in a big box bookstore, and if I didn't feel like I had to have it immediately, I pulled up Amazon on my phone, found the book to be significantly less expensive, knew I could have it on my doorstep in two days with Prime shipping, and placed the order—while inside the bookstore. (I do *not* do this if I'm in an indie bookstore. I'm happy for them to take my money all day long!)

If you're self-published and you want to get your books carried by an independent bookstore (which several of my authors have successfully done) or you wish to have a signing or other event at a local independent bookstore, you can upload your book to IngramSpark, which allows the bookstore to purchase wholesale from Ingram. Or you can offer to sell copies directly to the bookstore (that you purchased at your author pricing from Amazon), offering them the standard 55 percent discount and a willingness to buy back any that haven't sold after ninety days. Many independent bookstores will also carry local authors' books on consignment, which means that you give them a supply of books and aren't paid until the books are sold.

PUBLISHING

CHAPTER 24

PUBLISHING MODELS

I recognize that the title of this book is *Write the Damn Book Already,* not *Publish the Damn Book Already.* But the topic of publishing comes up so often (and usually well before someone has even started writing) that I know it's in your best interest to understand this part of the process so that you don't let the lingering questions slow you down you any more than they already have.

The truth, the whole truth, and nothing but the truth: I had to consume a (large) bowl of Graeter's mint chocolate chip ice cream before sitting down to write this section. This is the topic about which I've had hours and hours (and hours) of conversation over the years with just about everyone, from *New York Times* bestselling authors to independent authors to independent publishers and everyone in between. The parameters used to designate various publishing approaches vary (especially when we start talking about vanity versus hybrid versus independent versus professional publishers). It's a hot topic, and my goal isn't to sway you one way or another when it comes to how and with whom you publish your book. My goal is simply for you to have a better understanding of how it all really works so you can ask the right questions upfront in order to make the best decision for you and have your expectations met (if not exceeded) from the get-go.

TRADITIONAL PUBLISHING

Traditional publishing is the paradigm that most authors aspire to (at least initially). It's the one where you get a "big" publishing house (think HarperCollins, Penguin Random House, or Simon & Schuster) to purchase the print rights (and sometimes other rights) to your book. Publishing houses that operate under the traditional model offer an advance to their authors, along with a team of publishing professionals who tackle the book editing, cover design, interior formatting, distribution, marketing, sales, and other aspects of the publishing process. In exchange, they retain a (large) portion of author earnings and typically have large input (if not outright say) over the book's final content, cover design, and marketing plan (if there is one). Traditional publishers also don't typically accept unsolicited submissions from authors, preferring to be presented with proposals from literary agents with whom they've created relationships.

When you're published traditionally, you can expect the white-glove treatment, to be sent on a massive worldwide book tour, and for every Barnes & Noble on either side of the Mississippi to carry your book. Because that's how traditional publishing works across the board, right? Sadly, no.

In most cases, signing on with a traditional publisher is not an easy or quick feat. It's also not necessarily the road you want to take, even if, right this very minute, it's the one you're wildly committed to. No publishing approach is inherently "bad" (except one, which I'll get to), but not understanding what each represents and the pros and cons of each can lead to disappointment and frustration.

Getting a traditional publisher usually starts with finding an agent, so many people who are writing a book (or considering doing so) post in forums or on social media, wondering how to embark upon this process. In reality, few of these people really know what they are asking or why, and that fact poses the greatest challenge. After all, if we assume that the next step after writing a book is finding an agent, but don't know why that's our preference and what the process looks like, we're more than a bit likely to make a misstep.

It's like saying, "I want a new car, so I'm just going to go to the dealership down the road," without having looked into it enough to know that the dealership down the road requires a minimum $10,000 down payment and only sells neon orange cars. If you are prepared to put that amount down and are dying for a neon orange car, it's the right option for you. But if you want to put zero down and are committed to a white car, knowing in advance that they don't offer what you desire will save you time. And time is as valuable as money, if not more so.

When considering the oft-desired white-glove treatment and massive book tour, for some authors who have a proven concept and a huge platform, it *can* work that way. And, of course, there are new authors with incredible agents working on their behalf who sell the rights to their books to the "big guys" every year. Many of those authors have great experiences, and many others don't. That's no different, by the way, from any other industry. Some approaches work wonderfully for some people, and some people wouldn't touch those same approaches with a thirty-foot pole.

Aspiring authors have great hopes when it comes to the idea that a "real" publisher will do the marketing and selling for them. But far more often than not, publishers don't sell books, authors do (as do bookstores—especially indies—if you're carried by one). No matter what publishing paradigm you choose, please be ready to grow a reader list and be persistent and patient when it comes to getting your work out there. A rough estimate suggests that there are more than 33,000,000 book titles currently for sale through Amazon. Thirty-three *million*! If you don't have a strong intention to continue making your target readers aware of your book's existence, it will quickly become blindingly clear what it feels like to be the proverbial needle in a haystack. A press release or quick social media post from any publisher—including one of the Big Five—won't cut it. Post-Covid especially, the publishing industry is drastically changing, especially for authors who aren't considered to be a "sure thing."

Just because a publishing house isn't one of the most recognized imprints doesn't mean it isn't legitimate. It's important to note that while people think of the Big Five publishing houses when the term "traditional publisher" is mentioned, there are a number of reputable smaller traditional publishers popping up these days, my favorite of which at present is Zibby Books, run by the inimitable Zibby Owens. She's put together a publishing model that's truly disruptive and author-centric, and you don't have to look much further than the authors whose books she's acquired to see how thrilled they are and supported they feel to be published by and partnered with her.

As I've acknowledged multiple times, I've not been traditionally published. I've also never said that I wouldn't ever go that route if the right opportunity and terms presented themselves. I have many friends who are traditionally published, and their experiences vary, not just from author to author but from book to book. I know of some authors who had a wonderful experience having their first book in the hands of a traditional publisher, but their second was a disaster. I also know of authors who have always been with traditional houses and would never consider anything else. And I know of authors who were traditionally published way back when it was the only option but have since formed their own publishing house or decided to publish with a hybrid/professional publisher (also sometimes referred to as a publishing services company).

The pros of traditional publishing are probably relatively obvious, however a few of the aspects of this model that seem like pros are actually cons once you understand how the business really works. One of the pros includes the prestige that comes with being able to say, "My book was published by one of the Big Guys," which I won't deny for a single moment. The other pros include the *perception* of the big advance, start-to-finish handholding, and help with marketing and distribution. These three aspects of traditional publishing are the ones that most often appeal to authors but are a wee bit misunderstood.

The advance (which is just that—an advance against future earnings) is typically not terribly large for a new author, especially one without a massive and engaged following, because the publishing house has no idea whether or not the book will sell. For first-time authors, the average advance is reported to range between $2500 and $5000—obviously not enough on its own to allow you to retire and move to a Greek island anytime soon. It's usually paid out in thirds—the first third when the contract is signed, the second when the book gets through editing, and the third when the book is published. You will also give fifteen percent of that advance to your literary agent, who has absolutely earned it by finding you an editor willing to take on the book in the first place! The good agents put their hearts into every single book they agree to take on. They make exactly zero dollars until a book sells to a publishing house, a fact many authors don't consider. They work entirely on commission, and for each book they're able to sell, there's a handful of others they aren't.

When it comes to hand-holding and white-glove treatment, most people don't realize that authors have control over very little once their book has been acquired by a traditional publishing house. In their defense, the publishing house is running a business, and their focus is book sales. So they're going to decide, based on their experience, how the book needs to look and sound in order to have the best chance of selling to the highest number of people. Many times, authors feel that the book that finally comes out doesn't fully resemble the book they initially wrote, which feels uncomfortable and certainly can make the book harder to promote.

Finally, marketing and distribution are areas people really don't understand when it comes to the ins and outs of the process in the traditional publishing world. Bookstores today are more protective than they've ever been of their retail space. Every book matters, because they need every book to sell. With over a million new titles being published every year, bookstores of course cannot put a copy of every one of them on their shelves. Publishing houses have sales personnel who work with the bookstores to encourage them to stock certain books, and obviously, reputable names are going to command the majority of the shelf space.

How much marketing support a book gets from a traditional house tends to be a bit hit or miss. Their marketing budgets are thin (this became even more apparent during the recent Department of Justice's bid to block Penguin Random House from acquiring Simon & Schuster), and to which books they go is often determined by their expectations about which books will generate the highest returns. According to authors signed to traditional houses, which books get the highest marketing budgets seems to be determined by what side of the bed the marketing department head woke up on some days. And yet, I recently spoke with an author who is published by a traditional house and who is ecstatic about the level of marketing support she's receiving from her team there. So again, experiences vary.

The time from having a book acquired by a traditional publishing house to it actually being available for purchase is often upwards of two to three years. Of course there are books that are fast-tracked, but once again, that's typically reserved for the books publishers know will sell by the truckload because the author already has a long, proven track record. Once you figure in the time to query and sign with an agent, the time the agent takes identifying an editor interested in purchasing the book, and the time you're working with the editor and then getting the book into the queue for publishing, the overall timeline can get long in a hurry. This isn't ideal for many authors who want their book to be on the market sooner than later in order to help them get the word out about a new or growing business venture, or to speak their truth when it comes to a pressing societal issue.

INDEPENDENT PUBLISHING

Both hybrid and vanity publishers (sometimes also referred to as indie publishers, small press publishers, or professional publishers) make up the many publishing houses that are not part of a larger conglomerate and do not operate under a traditional model. There are a lot of them—so many, in fact, that they make up nearly half the market share of the industry. Many of them operate wonderful businesses with integrity, yet far more do not. It's therefore important to know what questions to ask and what red flags to be on the lookout for.

Hybrid Publishing

Hybrid publishing is a model whereby an author pays a publishing house to do the publishing legwork—including editing, cover design, interior formatting, and distribution channel setup—while retaining final say over the edits, title, cover design, interior layout, and retail price. It is reasonable to refer to these companies as publishing services companies, and the author would still be considered a self-published/indie author. The cost to work with a hybrid publishing company is likely to fall somewhere between $1,500 and $50,000. Several of the bigger, more well-known traditional publishing houses offer what they refer an author-financed model: Hay House has Balboa Press, and Simon & Schuster has Archway Publishing.

Some hybrid publishers take no profit off sales, while others take 15 percent (or more). Some houses pay author royalties every month; others pay them every quarter. Some make it easier than others for authors to order books for events or promotion, but almost all of them upcharge when an author does so. Some will claim that their services are "free" in exchange for 50 percent of sales, which could, on its own, cause them to be considered a variation on traditional publishing, but they also require that at least 2,000 (or more) copies are ordered within a certain period of time. If that doesn't happen, the author is required to purchase that number of books (including the publisher's markup) to ensure that the publisher profits from the arrangement. That little caveat makes the publishing company *not* traditional.

You may be thinking, "Not a problem! I can probably sell 2,000 copies!" However, the lynchpin is that the sales often have to come from the publisher's website directly, not from another distributor such as Amazon. It's not easy to get 2,000 people to purchase a book at full price (plus shipping) from a publisher when she can purchase it from Amazon and have it in two days (with no shipping and sometimes less expensively than retail price, as Amazon often plays with pricing to find the sweet spot where the most books are selling. When you make money, Amazon makes money!).

When you don't meet your publishing contract's sales quota and you're on the hook to purchase a truckload of books (that you now have to store somewhere), the bill can be five figures. So in the end, their service wasn't truly "free" after all.

Again, this isn't to suggest that this model is "bad." Some business owners are happy to invest in 2,000 copies of their book to sell at events or give away to media or use for other promotional activities. What's important is simply that you understand *exactly* what you're signing up for with each publishing model and know what questions to ask each publishing house/company so your expectations are set and you aren't blindsided later on.

One of the reasons people work with a hybrid publishing house (beyond their experience and know-how when it comes to taking a book through the paces to publication) is to have that house's imprint on the back cover (the imprint is the name of the publishing house, such as Simon & Schuster). Having what feels like a "real" publishing house's imprint on their book gives a lot of authors an initial sense of validation. However, it's important to note that very few readers pay attention to who published the book, and even the Big Five houses have so many divisions these days that few people recognize any of those divisions as part of a "big house."

A strong pro of the ethically operating hybrid publishers (when compared to most vanity publishers, which I'll discuss next) is the fact that they're typically selective about what they publish. They don't accept any and every manuscript that comes across their desk. They are clear about the services they provide to authors while believing in the books they bring to market, and they value partnership with their authors. They do the heavy lifting to ensure that a book is produced professionally while allowing authors more control over time to market and creative assets (cover design, title and subtitle selection, and final edits). They also typically *do not* proactively solicit authors, claiming to have discovered their book (or the book they are about to publish) and offering to publish it (for a fee). If you receive an email or other correspondence from a publishing house soliciting your business, it's a *huge* red flag, in my opinion.

In 2018, David Goggins made an enormous splash when he turned down a traditional publishing offer with a reported $350,000 advance, because he wanted to retain full control over his content, distribution, and marketing. His book, *Can't Hurt Me: Master Your Mind and Defy the Odds*, (which was published through Lioncrest Publishing, a hybrid/professional publisher) has done pretty well (hear the sarcasm). As of this writing, his book has more than 59,000 reviews on Amazon, averaging 4.8 stars. It's been reported that he's earned more than twice what he would have earned had he signed with that traditional publisher, given the profit margin he maintained as an independent author, as opposed to giving the publishing house 90 percent of the profit. To be fair, if someone is taking 100 percent of the risk, I don't think it's wholly unreasonable for them to take a large percentage of the profit, but when a book ends up doing exceedingly well, it's not uncommon for an author to feel a bit saddened by the fact that someone else is making the lion's share of the money off their intellectual property.

The cons to hybrid publishing tend to show up only when an author doesn't know what questions to ask and, therefore, makes incorrect assumptions about how the process with a particular hybrid publisher works when it comes to who controls the KDP account the book is loaded under, whether a percentage of sales is retained by the publisher, how often royalty payouts are made, and what kind of marketing support the author will receive.

Vanity Publishing

Many authors are initially excited to receive an email from a "publishing house" expressing interest in the book they either just published or are about to publish. I've had clients say, "I just heard from so-and-so at a publishing house. They saw my social media post about writing a book, and they're interested!" Not wanting to completely rain on their parade, I enthusiastically respond, "That's great! Who is the publisher?" Most often, the author responds with the name of a publishing house I've never heard of (which, in and of itself, isn't at all a red flag). What *is* a red flag is the fact that they solicited you to hire them to publish your book (and, more than likely, tried to win you over with all kinds of bells and whistles such as marketing assistance and website creation).

This model is referred to as vanity publishing, and it's my least favorite approach ever, because it's typically a money grab for the publishing company and an extremely disappointing experience for the author. If a publishing company solicits you to sign an author-financed publishing contract, it's safe to assume that it's a vanity publishing house.

Vanity publishers function similarly to hybrid publishers in many respects, but more often than not, authors end up extremely disappointed with their services. For one thing, vanity publishers are usually willing to publish absolutely anything by anyone willing to pay them. As a result, they have gobs of clients, sub-par service, and a catalog many authors aren't proud to be included in. Once your book is published (and they're finished collecting money from you), they tend to check out.

These companies masquerading as publishers tend to troll Facebook groups to find new prospects. While they suggest that they want to help you make your book a massive success, in truth there is little they want to do besides take many thousands of your dollars in exchange for promises they have no intention of making good on. They also typically retain some rights, take a portion of earnings off the backend, and occasionally disappear altogether, making it incredibly difficult to get your IP back from them.

I recently re-published a book for an author whose vanity publisher was acquired by a new company. The new company honored none of the agreements the authors had with the previous company, so the author had to pay *more* money to have the rights to her own material reverted to her. The previous company was on the verge of bankruptcy when she signed with them (which is why she never received a penny of her royalties), and we learned that the Chinese translation rights had been sold to a publisher in China without the author's knowledge or consent (she therefore didn't see a dime of those earnings either). It was a mess, and I'm hearing about it happening more often these days, which is incredibly unfortunate.

While I'm aware of a number of solid, reputable hybrid/professional publishers, I'm hard-pressed to identify a vanity publisher I'd recommend. They tend to be business-focused, not book- or author-focused, and more often than not, the authors who work with them end up quite disappointed.

Key Questions to Ask If You Are Considering an Hybrid Publisher/Publishing Services Company

- What is the process for ordering author copies, and is there an upcharge from the wholesale/printing price when I do?
- If the publisher offers website creation, is that a private website or simply a page on the publisher's site?
- Do I have to use an editor from the publishing house? If so, what is the process of editor selection/assignment?
- What is the expected timeline from finished edits to published book available for purchase?
- Where is the book uploaded for distribution?
- Is the book loaded to the publishing house's account on KDP (or other distribution channels) or the author's?
- If the book is listed under the publishing house's distribution account, what is the process for changing the price of the book post-publication if desired for sales or promotions? Also, what is the process for changing the book description, categories it's listed

under, or keywords?

SELF-PUBLISHING
(Sometimes referred to as Author Publishing/Indie Publishing)

This is the model I can speak to most confidently because it's what I've been doing since 2003 and helping people with since 2017. Self-publishing or hybrid publishing with a reputable publisher remain my most recommended options for the majority of new authors in the nonfiction and memoir space.

Self-publishing is the model whereby you take full responsibility for everything. It can feel quite overwhelming at first, but it's executed far more easily than expected once you know what to do first, second, and third. While the process of how to write a book isn't always a straight path, the process of publishing one is. In short, you write the book, then hire an editor. Once the book has gone through multiple rounds of editing and is declared "ready to go," you'll need to work with a proofreader; hire a cover designer and interior formatter; acquire ISBNs (the UPC code for books); and upload to KDP (Amazon) and possibly IngramSpark, should you desire distribution outside Amazon.

It is entirely possible to self-publish a book that is indistinguishable in quality from any *New York Times* bestseller. Of course, that doesn't guarantee that it will *become* a NYT bestseller. That part is the author's responsibility—whether they're self-published, independently published, or with a traditional publishing house. If you don't believe me, have a look at any well-known author whose book is being released soon by a traditional house. They're doing (and they're expected to do) a huge amount, if not all, of their own promotion. No matter who you publish with, and no matter what they promise you, you'll more than likely be doing the vast majority of your own publicity (at least, if you want to sell enough books to earn out your advance or earn back your investment or simply make as much of an impact as possible, which is most people's biggest goal).

The first course I created, Publish A Profitable Book, walks authors who wish to self-publish through the entire publishing process, step-by-step, from finding a great editor all the way to holding their published book in their hands. Because people then wonder what the heck to do to get that incredible book they're holding in their hands into the hands of as many people who will love it as possible, I created my third course, From Manuscript to Market, which gives authors my exact 12-day launch strategy, complete with email templates, social media templates, and day-by-day "do this, then do that" instructions. Writing a book isn't a linear process, but publishing and launching it are, and there's no reason for it to be any more overwhelming than necessary!

The publishing industry can feel mind-boggling, but it doesn't need to. There is no one "right" approach for everyone. Nothing is one-size-fits-all. The key is knowing what's most important to you, what's realistic, and what thoughts you're having about each publishing model that are holding you back (or outright false) in order to determine which approach is right for *you* for *this* book. You can always change your mind for the next one! Authors do it all the time.

CHAPTER 25

THAT'S ALL SHE WROTE!

You now have everything, almost literally, that you need to write powerful, thought-provoking nonfiction or memoir. You have a process to help you get solid in the foundation of what you're writing, for whom, and why; an understanding of how to navigate the most common "But what if..." thoughts likely to show up during the course of your journey; and greater clarity on the various ways to get your book published and into the world.

It is my great hope that this information has only further fueled your desire to write the damn book, as well as your belief that you absolutely *can* do so. The world needs your story. We need your unique insights. Hearing others' stories is one of the greatest (if not *the* greatest) ways we connect with and learn from one another as human beings in order to grow into the grandest version of who each of us truly is.

Telling your story and sharing your message will undeniably expand you into the next greatest version of yourself. The grace to work through the pieces that feel a bit crinkly at first is a gift you give yourself, even before you give it to others. It's an incredible act of self-love, self-acceptance, and self-respect.

Should you have further questions about the book-writing or publishing process, or wish to have more support as you engage in either, I have a library of downloads, free workshops, and paid programs available to assist you. You can find all of them through PublishAProfitableBook.com. It would be my absolute honor and pleasure to help you get your story or message out into the world.

Before we part ways, make me one promise. Even if we don't work together further to get your book written or published, even if you hire another writing coach altogether, promise me that you'll let me know when your book is available for purchase so I can cheer you on *and* add it to my own to-be-read pile, devour it, and learn from you. I don't believe that you're reading this book by accident, just as I don't believe we read anything by accident.

Maybe you're reading this because the universe knows that your message will impact *my* life.

Your story matters.

Your message matters.

Everything you need is already inside you.

Now close this book, get yourself in front of that blinking cursor, and write the damn book already.

ABOUT THE AUTHOR

Elizabeth Lyons is a 6x author, book writing coach, book editor, and host of the Write the Damn Book Already podcast. She's passionate about helping aspiring authors untangle the process of book writing and publishing so they can stop procrastinating-slash-overthinking, and get on with writing, publishing, and launching their incredible story!

A mom of 5, she is obsessed with (decaf) coffee, gluten-free cupcakes, and consistently remodeling her already-perfectly-fine house. She lives in Arizona with whichever of her kids happen to be home at any given point in time.

www.ElizabethLyons.com
www.PublishAProfitableBook.com

ACKNOWLEDGMENTS

To Grace, Jack, Henry, George, and Nina. For being my greatest inspiration and motivation for doing every damn thing already.

To Drew Linsalata. For making the flow of this book exceptionally better and for being such a light in the lives of so many who are forever better for your gift of Compelling Compassion.

To Zibby Owens. For being one of the strongest author advocates around. And an incredibly kind human being.

To everyone who's ever trusted me with their story or will do so going forward. The honor was, is, and will forever be mine.

And to every author who's ever inspired me to keep writing, reading, and growing (the list would fill another book entirely). Your words change my life daily, and I'm ferociously grateful.

www.ingramcontent.com/pod-product-compliance
Lightning Source LLC
Chambersburg PA
CBHW020229130626
46549CB00005B/1803